Spirit Boards
For Beginners

Photo © Sarah O'Brien

About the Author

Alexandra Chauran (Issaquah, WA) is a second-generation fortuneteller, a third degree elder High Priestess of British Traditional Wicca, and the Queen of a coven. As a professional psychic intuitive for more than a decade, she serves thousands of clients in the Seattle area and globally through her website. She is certified in tarot and has been interviewed on National Public Radio and other major media outlets. Alexandra is currently pursuing a doctoral degree, and can be found online at EarthShod.com.

To Write to the Author

If you wish to contact the author or would like more information about this book, please write to the author in care of Llewellyn Worldwide Ltd. and we will forward your request. Both the author and publisher appreciate hearing from you and learning of your enjoyment of this book and how it has helped you. Llewellyn Worldwide Ltd. cannot guarantee that every letter written to the author can be answered, but all will be forwarded. Please write to:

Alexandra Chauran
℅ Llewellyn Worldwide
2143 Wooddale Drive
Woodbury, MN 55125-2989

Please enclose a self-addressed stamped envelope for reply,
or $1.00 to cover costs. If outside the USA, enclose
an international postal reply coupon.

Spirit Boards

For Beginners

The History & Mystery
of Talking to the Other Side

ALEXANDRA CHAURAN

Llewellyn Publications
Woodbury, Minnesota

FIRST EDITION
First Printing, 2014

Book format by Bob Gaul
Cover photo and design by Lisa Novak
Editing by Laura Graves

Llewellyn Publications is a registered trademark of Llewellyn Worldwide Ltd.

Library of Congress Cataloging-in-Publication Data
Chauran, Alexandra, 1981–
  Spirit boards: the history & mystery of talking to the other side/
Alexandra Chauran.
       pages cm
  Includes bibliographical references.
  ISBN 978-0-7387-3874-1
1. Ouija board. 2. Spiritualism. I. Title.
  BF1343.C43 2014
  133.9'325—dc23
                                        2013042271

Llewellyn Publications
A Division of Llewellyn Worldwide Ltd.
2143 Wooddale Drive
Woodbury, MN 55125-2989
www.llewellyn.com

Printed in the United States of America

Other books by Alexandra Chauran

Crystal Ball Reading for Beginners
Faeries and Elementals for Beginners
Have You Been Hexed?
Palmistry Every Day
So You Want to Be a Psychic Intuitive?

contents

This book is dedicated to my ancestors,
on whose shoulders I stand: Grandma Bessie;
Grandpa Nick; my dad, Roy Pawlucki, who is proud
of my writing even though he never saw it in life;
and all those whose names are yet unknown.

*C*ome on, it's just a game!" The other boys looked down at Tommy as he stood poised at the tree house ladder, ready to descend and run away from the Ouija board and the scary noises of his friend's backyard at night. Two other faces leered over flashlights as Josh and Anthony urged him to stay. "You aren't chicken, are you?" They weren't allowed to use candles, but the flashlights cast an eerie glow, making them look like demons summoned by the Ouija board itself.

Tommy's mother wouldn't even let him play with a Magic 8-Ball to answer questions. She claimed the fluid-filled plastic orb was evil, so he was pretty sure she wouldn't want him using the Ouija board to talk to spirits. That night, he had already seen the planchette move on its own, and he had heard ghosts rapping on the wood outside the tree house. He definitely didn't want to push his luck any further. Wordlessly, he turned his *head and escaped the tree house, bare feet pounding into the soft earth, fleeing to the welcoming light cast by the windows of his friend's house. Let Josh and Anthony risk their own souls. It was their choice. Tommy didn't want any part of that evil.*

Similar scenarios have played themselves out in countless club houses, basements, and bedrooms around the world. Even though the ink is applied to a Ouija board by printers in a factory—not by witches or magicians—and the plastic message indicator called "the Mystifying Oracle Planchette" is molded just like any other toy, the game is feared. Ouija, which now glows in the dark, is packaged, shipped, and then displayed in toy stores, sitting rather unremarkably alongside other board games. Generations of children and adults have been tickled, amazed, and frightened by incredible and downright creepy Ouija board experiences. The humble manufacturing process of the Ouija board doesn't mean that magic and witchcraft don't exist; there are still people today who practice witchcraft, which is the art of magic. The modern definition of "magic" states that it is both an art and a science of creating change in the world that aligns with the practitioner's will.

Prepare for a wild ride through the practices that predate the Ouija board such as channeling, automatic writing, and similar board-based and dowsing instruments found in cultures around the world. Explore the early origins of talking boards and spirit boards and their religious use by members of the Spiritualist Church. Learn how a succession of entrepreneurs and shrewd marketing men slapped a patent on an ancient tool and launched the phenomenon of the Ouija board, now an essential entertainment tool brought out at every American child's Halloween slumber party.

In the chapters ahead, several controversies that surround the Ouija board will be discussed. First, we'll view the Ouija board with a critical eye and ask a few skeptical questions. Do the spirits of the dead really have nothing better to do than move a plastic and cardboard toy? Or is it more likely that excited hands are just moving the planchette in accordance with subconscious cues from the brains of the people using the board?

Follow the Ouija board through history as we trace how it is tied to the boom of a mediumship fad of the late nineteenth century, in an unprecedented movement that explored supernatural phenomena. Unfortunately, it spawned some of the biggest hoaxes of the millennium, completely fooling audiences including a president of the United States. Many victims were parted from huge sums of money by fraudulent mediums.

The religious controversy will be discussed through the voices of people who use spirit boards as part of their own spiritual practice, as well as those who believe that the use of the Ouija board is forbidden by God himself. Astoundingly, this simple toy has inspired people to write novels and scripture— or alternatively, to destroy or discard the board itself out of fear.

Families from similar walks of life make very different choices about the Ouija board. Some parents and caregivers who provide children with access to learning materials and safe playthings shun the Ouija board as dangerous. Others believe that the Ouija board is nothing more than good, clean fun, and can share stories from their own childhoods about Ouija board games played with friends.

Finally, make sure you have enough lights on as you read the chapter filled with bone-chilling true stories of creepy experiences that happened to people while using the Ouija board. From startling revelations to terrifying physical phenomena, these are the real stories that people will never forget, and will give you pause to think. The board is laid out in front of you and the planchette points to YES. Will you proceed?

History of the Ouija Board

The Ouija board holds many mysteries, but it is no mystery why humans have always wanted to get in touch with the invisible and unknown. A uniquely human condition is the fear of the personality and memories of a lifetime disappearing after death. Within minutes of dying, brain connections that take a lifetime to form and represent cherished memories and personality begin to melt away, never to exist again. It seems like a terrible waste, and is definitely a terrifying prospect. Nobody knows whether their death will be painful or peaceful, quick or slow.

Along with other intelligent mammals like elephants, we also miss and honor our dead loved ones, wanting to find a way to make the relationship continue beyond death. Of course, all cultures and times have had ghostly experiences in which apparitions made their presences known by visually appearing and speaking aloud. However, people struggled with how to make communication with ghosts possible for everyone. What if Grandma's ghost simply never appeared to anyone after her death? Did that mean she was gone forever, or that she simply didn't have the opportunity or the inclination to chat? A method was needed to isolate the essence or spirit of a dead person in a specific place and time so that people could try to communicate with him or her.

People have been trying to communicate with spirits for many years. Channeling through Spiritualist or psychic mediums, automatic writing, alectryomancy in Rome, *fuji* spirit writing in China, and dowsing with a pendulum or a board are all methods that have been used for centuries.

Dowsing Boards

Pendulum dowsing becomes a bit more like a Ouija board when dowsing boards are included. A dowsing board is a surface upon which markings are written that show answers that a spirit can indicate. Dowsing boards eliminate confusion, since there can be a "yes" and a "no" written on the dowsing board. In general, rapid movement of any kind indicates that the marking on the board is being acknowledged by a spirit, while a pendulum that does not swing as it is held over different markings means that they are not meaningful to the spirit.

Dowsing boards can have lots of different content. For example, a chart of dates or an anatomical diagram can be shown on a dowsing board to allow the pendulum to indicate timing of events or origins of disease. A dowsing board can be less specific as well, resembling a Ouija board with lettering. There are entire books filled with dowsing board diagrams to help answer any questions that one might want to ask of the spirits. A Ouija board can be used as a dowsing board with a pendulum if the planchette is misplaced or not desired.

You can also make a dowsing board to use with your Ouija board planchette. With a piece of paper and a pen, you can make any diagram you wish that includes words, symbols, or pictures. If you ever had any frustration with the limitations of the letters and words on the Ouija board, now is your chance to improve upon the design. You can even use a different dowsing board for different questions on different subjects like love, money, health, or any matter that needs clarifying.

Planchette

The word "planchette" is French, and its modern form may have appeared in France around 1853. The planchette can take many forms, but is usually heart-shaped with the point most often leading the direction of movement. Planchettes usually have three points of contact. It may have three casters or three casters and a pen. Felt may be used instead of casters in order to facilitate a smooth gliding effect. A planchette can also have a single solid point of contact around a lens or hole that acts as an indicator, much like a magnifying glass.

Only the operator's fingertips are used on a planchette, and when it was adopted by the Spiritualist movement, it was only used by two people at a time. When a planchette holds a pen, it can act as a tool for automatic writing or can even produce drawings. The scribbles may need to be analyzed carefully in order to find any meaningful content.

Try this handy way to make a pen planchette: Grab a piece of paper, a felt-tip marker, and a drinking glass that is at least as long as the marker. Take the lid off the marker and drop it in the cup with the felt tip pointing up. Then, overturn the cup with the marker in it on top of the piece of paper. When two or more people put their hands on the glass, it can be slid across the paper as a planchette and the pen will draw a line. Use the pen planchette like a Ouija board to write letters or draw symbols or pictures. You'll not only have fun, but will be creating a visual record of your use of the planchette.

You may want to use a stack of paper so that when one page is full, you can slide it out from underneath your make-shift planchette and have a fresh one ready to go. Of course, the pen will slip around inside the cup, so if you want to make a more permanent planchette, I suggest putting a bit of molding clay in the bottom of the cup to secure the pen. That way, your messages may be more clear and less time-consuming to receive.

Talking Boards and Spirit Boards

The first time a planchette was put to an alphabet on a board, the arrangement was not yet called a Ouija board. Though to some extent the Ouija board has become a common name, just like the Sony Walkman became a generic name for any portable tape player and Kleenex became the name for any tissue, the generic name for the type of device branded the Ouija board is called a "talking board" or less commonly "spirit board."

Before the Ouija board was born, talking boards had been in existence for millennia, and it's possible that even Confucius and Pythagoras used talking boards. And before talking boards came to be, planchettes existed on their own. Perhaps based on ancient Chinese fuji, these devices came to find renewed use in America during the Spiritualist movement. After Spiritualist Churches and famous mediums began to bring channeling into the public eye, a less organized movement began in nineteenth-century homes all over the country.

People started using planchettes to produce evidence of the spirit world themselves, right in their own homes without the use of a Spiritualist medium. Later, in order to make the movements of the planchette more meaningful, homemade talking boards were crafted for the planchettes so the spirits would be able to deliver messages more precisely.

Like the Ouija board, most talking boards contain all of the letters of the alphabet, the numbers zero through nine, and a simple "yes" and "no" printed upon them. Talking boards can be made of paper, wood, or even stone. Like the Ouija board, a planchette pointer is used with a light touch to spell out messages. Unlike the Ouija board, however, talking boards can be any shape, not just rectangular. The planchette can also vary in construction materials and shape, although the method of use remains the same.

Invention of the Ouija Board

It wasn't long before somebody thought to patent and mass produce a talking board. Attorney and inventor Elijah Bond got together with businessman Charles Kennard to draft the idea. On February 10, 1891, the Ouija board was issued U. S. Patent number 446,054. The first explanation for the board's name came from Charles Kennard, who claimed that a spirit told him through the board to call it *Ouija*, because it was an ancient Egyptian word for "good luck." However, manufacturer William Fuld later shared that the Ouija board was simply named after the French word for yes, *oui*, combined with the German word for yes, *ja*. The original name had even been called the "Oriole Talking Board" before he settled on "Ouija, the Mystifying Oracle."

Although Elijah Bond and Charles Kennard are both given attribution for inventing the Ouija board, the first Ouija boards were stamped with only William Fuld's name, along with the word "inventor." And while the Ouija board was marketed during his time with the words "Original Ouija board," William Fuld didn't limit his investment to the Ouija board as the only talking board. He trademarked the "Oracle" in 1902 and made a cheaper "Mystifying Oracle" in 1919 to try to generate additional money out of the Ouija board earnings. He also trademarked the names "WE-JA," "Egyptian Luck Board," and "Hindu Luck Board," just in case.

Once mass production started, competitors flooded the market with knock-off Ouija boards, causing William Fuld to fight many legal battles in order to protect the name of the original Ouija board. William Fuld aggressively protected his interests and went after anybody who tried to use the Ouija board name. He applied his energy to creating several spin-off products in order to profit further from the Ouija board's success, including branded Ouija board jewelry and even a special Ouija oil that was supposed to cure rheumatism. By the 1920s, William Fuld claimed to have reached millionaire status from the Ouija board alone. Later, in 1967, the Ouija board was catapulted to America's favorite board game, even above Monopoly. And by 1971, more than ten million Ouija boards were sold in the United States alone, which means that an estimated twenty million or more Americans may have been trying them out for the first time. As the popularity of talking boards soared through the next few decades, it gradually became evident that children loved to play with the Ouija board for divination, conversation with spirits, or simply to scare each other.

Though he pulled many publicity stunts to generate curiosity about the Ouija board, William Fuld could not have predicted the publicity generated by his own bizarre death. He accidentally fell from a three-story building when leaning on a railing in 1927. His family continued to own his business, the Southern Novelty Company. When Fuld's estate finally sold the business in 1966, the decision was made for all of its assets to go to Parker Brothers, which was later acquired by the toy company Hasbro in 1991.

Other Contemporary Brands of Talking Boards

Though not as enduring as the Ouija board, other brands of talking boards are plentiful on the market today, often with creators selling more than one talking board type branded differently for marketing purposes, made for different types of sessions, or simply colored and styled differently to appeal to different customers.

For example, the Psychic Circle, Enchanted Spell Board, and Pathfinder Talking Board kits are all made by Amy Zerner and Monte Farber. With different brand names for what is functionally the same product, each kit comes with a self-help instruction book and a square board with a circular design that includes letters of the alphabet as well as astrological signs and other symbols. The packaging and slight difference in the style of the designs may appeal to different consumers who might use the board to solve complex problems through the divinatory symbols.

Comic book writer Mike Mignola, creator of the Hellboy character and comic series, also created art for a talking board. The Hellboy talking board is designed to look more like the Ouija board, being rectangular in shape and having the same content. However, it is marketed primarily to collectors, who are unlikely to use the board as their main connection with the spirit world or for a party game. Likewise, there is a Buffy the Vampire Slayer: Conversations With Dead People talking board of similar design, presumably also targeted to collectors and memorabilia fans.

Auction and handmade spiritual supply websites are also flooded with personalized talking boards that are often made of painted or burned wood and given mystical designs or themes. More elaborately designed talking boards made from cast resin and decorated with trees, vines, and pentacles are marketed specifically to Neopagans and Wiccans who might use the board in personal spiritual practice for divination or ancestor worship.

The Original Purpose of the Ouija Board

The original purpose of the Ouija board wasn't for child's play, but it wasn't the serious business of the talking boards that spun off from the Spiritualist movement either. Rather, early

Ouija boards were relegated to adult parlor games for amusement during parties and small social gatherings. It wasn't until era of the First World War that the Ouija board was once again given a reputation for serious use with spirits by Spiritualist medium Pearl Curran. During wartime, many people were missing relatives who had disappeared or been killed in faraway lands, and the bereaved were desperate to reestablish contact. Pearl Curran showed that the Ouija board could also be used for divination, the practice of using a tool in order to receive messages or advice about the past, present, and future. Up until inventions like the Ouija board, the vast majority of divination tools required difficult interpretations of symbols or writing. With a Ouija board, any literate person could perform divination.

What Is a Ghost?

The concept of ghosts spans time, location, and cultures. Some religious practices that include the practice of honoring ancestors, such as Vodou, believe that everyone who dies can exist on earth afterwards as a ghost, in order to help one's descendants. Other faith traditions, such as some Neopagan and New Age spiritualities, state that a ghost is the spirit of a person who has been kept on earth to solve a problem or learn a lesson, or because they are in a state of confusion after suicide or a violent death. Some Christians believe that ghosts can exist on earth because they are being punished or put in limbo as a result of suicide. Whether it's due to fear or detachment, many Americans choose to explore ghosts through a simple game like the Ouija board.

I have interacted with many ghosts, but one incident changed the sort of questions I asked and what I do with the information.

I was visiting a beautiful beach town on the coast. In the early morning hours, I walked the docks, listening to the boats knocking against the wood and to the sounds of chains jingling. When I saw her, I was frightened that she was a living child. She seemed to rise up from the wood grain in a boat, but then appeared solid and living. A frightened little girl wearing a stained T-shirt and jeans looked at me with solemn eyes, as if I had caught her doing something wrong.

Still wondering what was going on but vowing to remain present in the moment, I stared at her, looking for things that might differentiate her from a living person. She rose and made her way to the edge of the boat without rocking it, and stepped barefoot onto the dock. I automatically knelt down on the cold damp planks. She approached me and whispered in my ear, asking if I could help her parents, and urging me to tell people where she was. At first, I thought she had a message for the parents, but she told me a story about drunken negligence, and I realized that this was something best told to law enforcement.

After my encounter with her, I could see that I had an ethical problem. I was given information about the missing body of a dead little girl, but I had to doubt my own eyes and ears. What if I wasted valuable police time? I could be arrested for making a false report. What if I was just being crazy? On the other hand, was it ethical to ignore the message I received? I wanted to help!

After consulting with some spiritually wise people in my life, I decided to anonymously report what I had learned to the police, explaining how I had received this knowledge, so that they could take that information with a grain of salt. In time, I received kind regards from law enforcement, and was given a deck of cards with information about cold cases printed on them. With that deck of cards and the Ouija board, I was well equipped to invite further messages from ghosts with mysteries yet to be solved.

What Is a Spirit Guide?

Spiritualist churches introduced the idea of a spirit guide. A spirit guide was originally a deceased person who would choose to remain a spirit in order to guide the living. The first spirit guides were often saints, ancient Egyptians, Chinese philosophers, or Native American sages. Later, the idea of a spirit guide was adopted by New Age and Neopagan practitioners and expanded to include nonhuman entities like angels, nature's elementals, totem animals, personifications of the higher self, or other sources of wisdom.

Some believe a spirit guide chooses one person and sticks with that person for life. So, the same spirit guide that a child might see in a dream would be the one that would help him or her as an elderly person. In other belief systems, it is thought that different spirit guides appear according to one's stage in life. So a child's spirit guide may depart when a person turns into an adult, and a new spirit guide may appear. Still others believe that there is an entire team of spirit guides assigned to each person. Whenever love problems arise in the person's life, the spirit guide whose expertise centers on relationships will appear, while another spirit guide may only come through when there is physical danger to be avoided.

How the Ouija Board Is Used

It's just a game, isn't it? If the Ouija board is just a game, you don't have to worry about complicated instructions for use. After all, instructions will be included with the game from the manufacturer, and you can be sure that they are simple enough for even an eight-year-old child to follow. If, however, you think that the Ouija board may have uses other than as a toy, there is a large body of lore and ritual structure from Western magical traditions and New Age practices that can aid you with spirit communication. Most Western magical traditions are derived from ceremonial magic, a practice used to command spirits and cast magical spells.

When to Use a Ouija Board

It is my goal in this chapter to provide you with the practical who, what, when, how, where, and why to use the Ouija board.

So, when should you use a Ouija board? I'd advise against using a Ouija board when feeling emotionally vulnerable, such as when experiencing great anger or fear, since it is possible that your emotions could affect your hand movements and your feelings could be further hurt by what you read. You might wonder how long after the death of a person you should wait before attempting contact with a Ouija board. Some cultures believe that three days' time must pass after death before a dead person has transitioned enough to become a spirit capable of communication.

Time of Year

There are two times of the year when it is believed that the veil between the worlds is at its thinnest, and spirit communication is least difficult. These points are midway between the equinoxes and solstices. The first time of the year is called Beltane in Neopagan traditions, and it is observed on May eve and the first of May. The second time is Halloween (called Samhain in Neopagan traditions), and it is on the last day of October and the first of November.

You might want to include a Ouija board for a Halloween party. Timing is important in many spiritual practices in which ghosts are believed to be bound to the earth. Since the earth is also bound by cycles of day, night, and seasons, paying attention may allow for easier spirit communication. Luckily, it isn't just twice a year when the Ouija board can be used efficiently. I'd like to go over the other times that can be used to boost your Ouija board's power.

Time of Month

The full moon is best for receiving spiritual messages. The three days preceding the actual date of the full moon also draw a lot of the moon's power. After the full moon, however, the power wanes quickly. So, it is better to choose a date three days before the full moon than even one day after. There is a specific time when each full moon peaks, just as there is a specific time for observing an eclipse or other celestial event. Check an astrological calendar to find out what time the moon peaks in your time zone so that you aren't accidentally just getting started as the moon is already waning. Rest and try not to use the Ouija board during the day of a dark (new) moon.

Time of Week

Each day of the week has correspondences that can align with your purpose for using the Ouija board. Most of our days of the week were named after Germanic deities because of their spiritual associations. Monday is moon day, Tuesday is Tiw's day, Wednesday is Woden's day, Thursday is Thor's day, Friday is Freya's day, Saturday is Saturn's day, and Sunday is the day of the sun. The spiritual associations for each day of the week are as follows:

- **Monday**—Generally a good day for using the Ouija board, Monday is best for questions about magic, fears, and cycles, and for contacting female spirits.

- **Tuesday**—Best for questions about health, anger, war, and disagreements. Tuesday is better for contacting male spirits.

- **Wednesday**—Another good day for using the Ouija board in general, Wednesday is best for questions about communication, legal issues, technology issues, education, travel, money, business, and signing contracts. Wednesday is better for contacting male spirits.

- **Thursday**—Best for questions about leadership, authority figures, politics, money, and employers. Thursday is best for contacting male spirits.

- **Friday**—Best for questions about love, sex, the home, and family, Friday is best for contacting female spirits.

- **Saturday**—Best for questions about death, sadness, job roles, saving money, and ending relationships. Saturday is good for contacting male spirits.

- **Sunday**—Best for questions about making money, succeeding at work or school, emotional or spiritual growth, and happiness. Sunday is best for contacting male spirits.

Time of Day

Traditionally, the Ouija board has been used at night. You can also use planetary hours to amplify the purpose of your use of the Ouija board, especially if you're not quite using it on the right day of the week or time of the month or year. Planetary hours are associations with each hour of the day and night that are tied to some traditional meanings of the planets from astrology and Greek and Roman mythology. To find out when the planetary hours occur at night, note the day of the week. At sunset, the hour begins for the planet that matches the day of the week as follows:

- **Monday**—Moon

- **Tuesday**—Mars

- **Wednesday**—Mercury

- **Thursday**—Jupiter

- **Friday**—Venus

- **Saturday**—Saturn

- **Sunday**—Sun

After the first hour passes, the hours cycle through the following planets over and over again in order until sunrise: Moon, Saturn, Jupiter, Mars, Sun, Venus, Mercury. So, on Saturday, the moment the sun sets, the hour of Saturn begins. An hour later the hour of Jupiter begins, and so on. Refer to the days of the week above and the meanings of the days of the week to see what questions are best to ask during each planetary hour.

It is nearly impossible to layer all of the correspondences perfectly. For example, it may be best to ask a love question on April 30 when the moon is just getting full on a Friday seven hours after sunset, but that is really unlikely to happen all at once. If you have a burning love question, you might just want to make sure the moon isn't new and wait until sunset on Friday. At the very least, you can try to hit the first hour of Venus after dark.

Self-Protection Before Using the Board

One of the most basic ways to protect yourself is to pay attention to your feelings; if you feel fearful or uncomfortable using the board, tell the spirits to leave immediately. There are several other ways to protect yourself before using the board. Before choosing which methods to use, you'll have to ask yourself what sort of things you fear and what you would need protection for. There are three potential things that people might want to avoid, so I will go over them here and some techniques to manage those factors. All the protection techniques can be used in concert for maximum comfort using the Ouija board, and some can be eliminated entirely if you don't feel that you need to avoid adverse effects—or if you actually desire the phenomena others might avoid.

(1) Protection from too much empathy or from feeling sick from the energies involved

Some believe the Ouija board uses the spiritual life energy that permeates the universe. This spiritual energy is sometimes called *chi* to distinguish it from the mechanical, chemical, or electrical energy of the material world. Chi is the force that makes magic happen and adds the sacred animation of life and spirit to things. It is chi that connects the entire universe and provides the framework within which the Ouija board can summon any spirit or answer any question.

There is a natural balance and flow of chi within every person. Spiritual activity, such as using a Ouija board, can create a temporary imbalance of chi that can feel unpleasant. An excess of chi can make a person feel jittery, agitated, dizzy, and nauseated. Too little chi can make somebody feel depressed, exhausted, confused, or light-headed. When chi flow is stuck, a person can feel physically ill. When chi flow is rampant and uncontrolled, a person can feel too much empathy such that they seem to take on negative emotions from people around them.

A procedure called "grounding" can be performed in order to maintain a healthy balance and flow of chi during and after using the Ouija board. Everybody naturally performs grounding subconsciously, but in times of stress or excitement, you can forget to ground in the same way you can catch yourself holding your breath. Also, the Ouija board may cause chi to flow into or out of the board, which can exacerbate an imbalance or improper flow inside a person's body. For this reason, I encourage everyone to ground, even if you are not afraid of the consequences. Grounding is a good general practice to remain calm and centered in all sorts of situations.

The most common procedure for grounding is to use visualization in order to stimulate chi flow into and out of the body. The best place to release or gain chi is through a connection with the earth established in your mind's eye. That way, the chi won't go elsewhere or into another person, inadvertently causing them the problems you want to avoid. Try closing your eyes and visualizing a connection with the earth. You can imagine roots growing out of your feet, tubes, anchors, or whatever draws your attention to your connection with the ground. You can use bare feet on dirt, or visualize the connection going through a floor, building, or even the air below an airplane. Once your connection is established, visualize pushing out negative, excess, or stuck chi harmlessly into the earth, and drawing up a fresh supply into your body, allowing it to swirl around freely and continuously. People see chi in their mind's eyes as light, smoke, water, or any other substance that can be seen to flow.

Grounding takes practice. When performed right, you will feel both calm and alert, so monitor your emotions and attention to gauge when the process is complete. Over time, your grounding skills will increase so you can do it almost instantly, but it may take quite a while to achieve at first. Try practicing grounding at least once a day, and then ground yourself before and after using a Ouija board. Some people find that the Ouija board doesn't work for them as well if grounding happens before use, so if you experience no ill effects from lack of grounding while using a Ouija board, you can safely wait until after using it to ground yourself.

(2) Protection from spirit possession

Plenty of people want to prevent spirit possession from occurring while using a Ouija board. After all, it sounds terrifying to hand over control of your body to a supernatural being. Complete spirit possession can cause memory loss during the use of the Ouija board, strange voices and actions produced by the possessed person, and maybe even dangerous behaviors such as self-harm.

However, keep in mind that one belief behind the mechanics of the Ouija board is that the participants are mediums channeling the spirit. With belief in the channeling theory, there is no way to effectively use the Ouija board to communicate with spirits without allowing a spirit into your body and mind to help direct your hands. At best, by preventing the spirits from accessing the Ouija board, your board could be used as an inspirational device to jog your own imagination or creativity. However, if you want to have some spirits channel their messages through you, you'll need to become comfortable with the idea of spirits accessing your body in some way.

However, there are some things you can do to prevent total spirit possession while channeling, limiting the spirit channeled to only give messages through the Ouija board, and putting safeguards in place against self-harm. First, if uncontrolled spirit possession and self-harm is something you have experienced before, make sure you don't use the Ouija board alone. Have a buddy in the room to keep you safe if you should lose control.

One Afro-Caribbean technique to prevent uncontrolled spirit possession is to stand or sit with your heels together and to cover your head with a white hat or scarf. These two precautions are thought to prevent malicious spirits from using the top of the head or the genitals as an entry point into the human body. In fact, a person who experiences mental illness is advised to wear a hat in the rain in that culture, just in case it is a spiritual affliction.

A Western technique for preventing total spirit possession is called "shielding." Shielding consists of the visualization of a barrier between your body and the rest of the universe to prevent penetration from unwanted entities. Keep in mind, however, that you will want some entities to reach you if you are using the board and believe in the channeling mechanism. First, however, I will go over a method of total shielding in case you are simply watching a board session and don't want to be involved in the channeling, or if you do not believe in the Ouija board's channeling mechanism and want to use it to record your own subconscious messages.

When I was taught shielding from spirit possession, my teacher called it the "garage door" because it was a barrier meant to be quickly closed when somebody else was experiencing spirit possession in a Neopagan ritual designed to call a goddess into the body of one priestess. The others participating in the ritual by watching would sometimes experience unwanted effects from the chi flowing out of the possessed priestess.

Once, when a goddess was being drawn down into a spirit possession of a priestess, I was watching and suddenly lost conscious awareness of my surroundings. Instead, I felt like I had been lifted up and out into the universe among the stars, and that I was drinking liquid in great gulps. When I returned to a normal state of awareness, my teacher first introduced me to the "garage door" as visualizing the barrier snapping into place, like a literal door coming down, a metal shield, or even an umbrella. Anything one can see in the mind's eye that can appear rapidly to come between the excess flow of chi and the person works.

If you do want to channel, however, using prevention techniques like the garage door may completely ruin the channeling experience. Instead, you'll need to visualize a more permeable shield, like a net, which only allows spirits through that have good intentions and will not attempt total possession. One common permeable shield visualization is to imagine that you are surrounded by a rainbow-colored cocoonlike shield or concentric bubbles. Depending on their intentions, you can imagine spirits can be stopped by any layer of the rainbow. The worst will stop at the first color they encounter, while some may bounce off halfway through if they are well-meaning but mischievous, or if they intend to produce a total possession experience. Only the most benign spirits that agree to your terms can pass through every color of the rainbow to reach your body.

(3) Protection from "evil" or negative entities using the Ouija board

A visualized shield around your body can protect you from negative entities controlling your hands through spirit possession. You can think about a shield as a personal chi bubble. However, if you worry about evil or negative entities moving the planchette directly without going through your body, you will have to create a larger sort of barrier that encompasses the entire board and all players and witnesses. Imagine a chi bubble encompassing a group of people or an entire room or building. The technique used to create this larger barrier is called casting a circle, and it is used in Western magical practices to keep entities out and hold chi in. For the purpose of protection while using the Ouija board, this circle will be modified to focus on maximizing protection from negative entities, allowing only good ones through.

Casting a circle is a ritual, which is needed to put the participants in the right frame of mind and to perform all of the right spiritual techniques in the right order in order to produce the desired effect. The theory behind casting a circle is to first clear away any negative entities that may already exist in a space, which is called "banishing," and then to create a boundary that seals off the space from the rest of the universe. After that, in many ritual practices, all the energies of the universe are called back in symbolically in a controlled manner, to create a microcosm, a tiny universe in which the Ouija board can be used safely and effectively. Typically, casting a circle involves many tools to move chi and to symbolically invoke important universal components.

The following is adapted from the popular ceremonial magic technique called the Lesser Banishing Ritual of the Pentagram. Since the circle you need to cast to protect yourself while using a Ouija board doesn't require all the bells and whistles of a ceremonial magic or Neopagan circle for casting spells or worshiping deities, many tools and elements of the ritual are omitted here for simplicity. However, if you happen to be already familiar with casting circles for other purposes, your own ritual will work fine. If you have never heard of casting a circle before, don't worry. This simplified but effective version is perfectly suitable for beginners or people just trying it out.

Steps to Casting a Banishing and Protective Circle

1. **Sweep the area**—Ideally, you will sweep the area in which you will use the Ouija board with a broom, even if it is outdoors or in a carpeted room. Walk in a counter-clockwise direction three times. The first time, sweep the floor, the second time, sweep the air around mid-level height, and the third time sweep the sky. If you don't have access to a broom, you can walk the circle space counter-clockwise while visualizing sweeping and pushing outward with your hands. The purpose of sweeping is to clear away any negative entities that may already naturally occupy the space in which you are going to be using the Ouija board.

2. **Banish and protect**—Stand in the center of the circle, about where the Ouija board will be placed, facing east. Ground and shield yourself. Draw a five-pointed star, (a pentagram, with your dominant hand and then plunge both hands through the center of the pentagram and breathe out in a slow and controlled manner. As you exhale, visualize any negative entities in the east fleeing from your circle. Withdraw your nondominant hand to your lips as if you were to shush those negative entities. With your dominant hand still extended, rotate ninety degrees to the right so you are facing the south. Repeat the gestures and visualizations in each of the remaining compass points of south, west, and north, and then complete your rotation so you are again facing east. Make sure you are grounded and shielded again. You may wish to light a candle at each of the four compass points to represent the protective energy that has been established.

3. **Define your circle space**—Make sure that everybody who will be using the Ouija board or observing can fit into the area and let everybody know where the boundaries of the protective circle will be. Explain that it is important that nobody leave the circle before it is taken down officially after the use of the Ouija board, because passing through the boundary may compromise its protective qualities. You may wish to make the boundary of the circle visible by drawing a line with chalk, salt, flour, rope, or a string on the ground. However, as long as everybody is informed about the boundaries, the line can be an invisible one. Walk around the circle area clockwise three times holding

out your dominant hand with your first two fingers to draw the line in your mind's eye. You are now ready to use the Ouija board.

Closing the Circle

It is important to officially close your banishing and protective circle before people pass through the boundary and after completing your play with the Ouija board. Removing the energy of the circle in the same way it was established prevents spirits from being attracted to the decaying energy as it loses its protective powers. In order to close the circle, you need simply to perform the steps in reverse order to reestablish a clearing of the room without the protective border.

1. **Remove the circle border**—Make a cutting motion with your hand in the west like a karate chop to pierce the boundary of your circle. Walk around the circle counter-clockwise three times with your dominant arm outstretched, visualizing the energy of the circle border being sucked back up through your arm and dispersed harmlessly into the earth through your feet.

2. **Perform the banishing pentagram gestures and visualizations again**—Just as you did in the circle casting, in order to allow the spirits that have gathered for the Ouija board to depart harmlessly in any direction they wish. If you used any candles, feel free to extinguish them at this point and turn on any ordinary lights that may be in the room.

3. **Sweep the area**—Pick up any rope or string you may have used to define your circle boundary, and sweep or vacuum up any salt or flour. Again, even if you have no visible circle boundary or broom, you can perform a sweeping motion in your mind and with your hands in order to disperse any other energies that collected in your circle area.

How to Use the Board Appropriately

If you are nervous about the Ouija board or new to it, always have two or more people using the planchette at a time. Not only does the use of more than one person prevent a solitary user from simply fooling himself or herself with the planchette and subconscious movement, it also has safety purposes. If a spirit possession were to happen to you, having a trusted other person around can be helpful. A buddy can make sure you don't wander into sharp objects or off into traffic, and can help keep you quiet and still so as to allow the spirit possession to pass without harm. There are those who believe that having more than one person using the planchette can prevent spirit possession entirely by confusing spirits with more than one potential body.

There is some debate on whether points on the board can be indicated by the window on the planchette or the planchette's point. Depending on the spirit or the person operating, either could be true. You can eliminate any ambiguity by simply putting a piece of tape over the window on the planchette so that you are only using its point to indicate points on the board. However, at the time of this writing, clear instructions to use the window are given by the packaging from the manufacturer, which indicate that the answers you seek are indicated in the planchette's window.

An alternative way to use the Ouija board I have observed is for one or more players to consciously move the planchette, but move it too quickly for a user to be able to hunt and peck the letters that they choose. Of course, users would still be able to pick out the yes or no answers, but the spelling would be impossible to control without being greatly experienced with the Ouija board such that one had memorized the location of each letter. The fast but conscious movement technique is good for infrequent users when a faster answer is preferred. Rotating the board for a user may also throw off any memorized letter locations.

A Typical Ouija Board Session Step-by-Step

There are a few formalities observed during the use of a Ouija board that may be bothersome at first, but can allow for greater speed and clarity in the long run. Imagine if you were one of those people who wrote an entire book using a Ouija board. You would want to know exactly what letters were highlighted as well as when one word ended and another began. Here are a few tips you can follow for more clarity once you get started, with steps for use based on the manufacturer's instructions:

1. All participants should agree on the questions to be asked. You can write down the questions before beginning, or consult with each other as you go along. Decide who will

be operators and who will be observers if more than one participant is present.

2. Remove the Ouija board from its box and any other coverings, and use a dry cloth to dust the board. Place the board on a small table within reach of all participants. A solitary operator can rest the board on his or her lap, or a pair can share the board between them on their laps.

3. Set the planchette in the center of the board. The planchette should return to the center of the board after each symbol is indicated.

4. Each operator should place two fingers lightly on the planchette and concentrate. Ask a question slowly. Questions should only be asked one at a time, and one to five minutes should allowed for the planchette to move.

5. If you have a third person or any willing additional observer, have him or her write down the messages as they appear. If there are only two of you, try to make an audio recording of the session, and transcribe the audio as soon as possible afterward so that the session is fresh in your memory.

6. If the planchette does not return to the center of the board after each symbol, and instead rushes directly from one letter to the next, simply ask for it to return to the center. If you find it difficult to tell when one word ends and another begins, ask for the planchette to move in a full circle in between words. If the planchette seems to land between letters, remind the spirit whether you are using the tip or the lens of the planchette as an indicator.

7.   If the planchette does not move or if the message makes no sense, wait out the maximum five minutes and then ask again or move on to another question.

8.   If the planchette moves to "goodbye," do not push that spirit to keep responding. It may mean that it is time to move on to another spirit or to end the session completely. If the answer "goodbye" persists when you ask for another session, have everybody take a break from playing with the Ouija board.

Lines of Questioning

The instructions that come with the Ouija board helpfully suggest that questions be decided ahead of time. Choosing questions before using the Ouija board is important for two reasons. First, it is important that every user and witness of the board be comfortable with the questions being asked, for ethical reasons. For example, if one person wants to call up the devil and the others do not, it would not be a pleasant Ouija board session, indeed, if the first person were to surprise the others with a question invoking the devil. Another good reason for deciding the questions ahead of time is for efficiency. When time is spent sitting and thinking of the next question, or asking a question that involves a lengthy spelled response with the letters, confusion and straying attention can result.

In order to increase efficiency, don't focus on the lettering section of the board right away. Try starting with yes or no questions, and then focusing on only the numbers of the board in order to limit everyone's attention to just a portion of the Ouija board. Finally, when everyone feels warmed up to how the planchette is moving, you can move on to spelling words, beginning with short, one-word answers.

Good "Yes" or "No" Questions to Start for a Spirit

- Is there a spirit present?

- Are you my spirit guide?

- Are you female?

- Are you male?

- Can we call upon the spirit of [name of deceased person]? Is he/she present?

Good Follow-Up Questions Focusing on Numbers for a Spirit

- In what year were you born?

- In what year did you die?

- How old do you feel?

- On a scale of 0–9, how much do you feel like answering questions for us right now?

- May we please speak with another spirit? Is another spirit present?

Good Short-Answer Spelled Questions for a Spirit

- What is the first initial of your first name?

- What is the first initial of your last name?

- Please spell your first name.

- Please spell your middle name.

- Please spell your last name.

- In what city were you born?

- In what city did you die?

Common Longer Answer Questions for When You Feel Warmed Up

- How did you die?

- Please tell me/us about the afterlife.

- Please tell me/us about divinity.

Easy-to-Use Divination Questions about Love

- What are the initials of a person who would be a good match for me to marry?

- Does [name] feel the same quality and intentions of love that I feel about him/her?

- I am choosing between two loves. What is the first initial of the one best for me?

- What age will I be when it is the right time for me to consider marriage?

- In what year will I meet my next potential boyfriend/girlfriend? What month? What day?

- Is it likely that my ex will choose to get back together with me?

- I'd like to pursue [*name*]. Please give me a word of advice for how to best achieve my goal.

Easy-to-Use Divination Questions about Career and Money

- I am choosing between two jobs. Give me the first letter in the name of the one best for me.

- In what year should I ask for a raise? What month? What day?

- What is the name of the city in which my next job will be located?

- In what year will I next have to change jobs?

Questions to Ask at the End of a Session

- Do you have any further messages for me/us?

- Is it okay with you if we say goodbye?

Ways You Can Accidentally Influence Yourself with the Ouija Board

"Cold reading" is the term sometimes applied when people are tricked into thinking that the Ouija board is revealing true information about themselves, their futures, or their deceased relatives when that is really not the case. Cold reading can be done by mentalists as a performance art, by friends as a game, or by scammers as a way to extract financial rewards. Rather than a single method, cold reading encompasses an entire wealth of methods that encompass the vast psychology of the human mind, and they can be used together or separately. We'll begin by starting out with some ways, aside from the ideomotor effect, that you might start out by tricking yourself without the other person even helping.

Setting the Stage—When you change your environment with a little bit of candlelight instead of incandescent or fluorescent light bulbs, your body and mind can't help but respond to it. If you make your surroundings seem mysterious or dangerous, your heart rate will increase and your brain will begin searching for things that explain your anxiety. Things that may seem ridiculous by the light of day will be highly credible when it is late and you are tired and spooked. An intimate atmosphere between you and one other person using the Ouija board can also take away the relaxing joviality of a large group.

Cooperative Interpretation—Setting up the two of you as members of a team trying to decipher one message can open yourselves up to being fooled. If you're both on the same side, and if you feel like you got a different message from the Ouija board than your partner did, you're more likely to think that you were simply mistaken. If you see one letter and your partner sees another, you will both tend to agree on the message that makes the most sense, assuming that the other data is extraneous.

Recollection—After your Ouija board session, certain things slip from your mind naturally. We don't remember every single second of our lives, particularly the boring ones. You will more easily forget the parts of your Ouija board session that were unremarkable or just plain wrong. You will, however, remember all of the startling revelations that were correct, even if they were few and far between. Over the course of one or many sessions, you'll collect far more amazing memories than boring ones. Every time you retell the story of your Ouija board experience, your story will become more interesting and surprising.

How Does the Planchette Work?

Few people think the planchette can be moved directly on its own by spirits. Skeptic Milbourne Christopher even performed an experiment in which users were blindfolded and the letters were rearranged. When he pointed a camera at the board to discover whether words could be formed, he was rewarded with complete gibberish. That evidence was consistent with the hypothesis that the planchette doesn't move on its own to places that it determines itself. Somebody has to be watching and moving the planchette.

The predominating theory behind the planchette is that the spirits move a person's hand by operating through some psychic part of the person's brain through channeling. Even though the person's hand is moving the planchette, he or she is largely unaware of the movement and cannot predict where it will go. So it follows that putting two skeptics at the planchette should ensure that the planchette does not work at all, right? Not necessarily. There is another psychological effect called the ideomotor effect at work that might make the planchette fool somebody who doesn't believe in spirits or even intend to move the planchette at all.

The *ideomotor effect* is the collection of small muscular movements that correspond with thoughts that form in the brain. The ideomotor effect is behind the small microfacial expressions that sometimes prove that somebody is lying. Even thinking of an extremely happy thought or an extremely sad one can tug at your smile or frown muscles for a moment, no matter how firmly you hold your poker face. Another example is if you find yourself mouthing along the words to a song very slightly, even if you do not intend to sing along.

The ideomotor effect can affect your hands as well. The ideomotor effect can be behind grimaces made when you think of a disgusting food, or the twitching of your hands when you think about undertaking a complicated manual task like tying shoelaces or cutting out a paper snowflake. Your whole body can be involved in the ideomotor effect when you watch a gymnast or a dancer on television and find yourself shifting your weight or holding your breath. When riding a bicycle, you want to be careful not to stare at any obstacles in your path, such as a pole. If you don't look in the direction you're going, and instead look at the barrier, you may find yourself colliding with the very thing that you are most worried about. Again, the ideomotor effect is at work, making sure that your body follows the thing upon which your brain and eyes are focused.

In fact, the Ouija board is not the only game that has made use of the ideomotor effect. I once played a computer game in which a skier appeared on the screen. The player was supposed to place a finger inside a sensor and simply think the direction in which the skier should go. I remember trying very hard not to move my finger and being amazed that the computer game seemed to read my mind. In actuality, my finger was making extremely small movements that were being picked up by the sensor.

Likewise, a person can be certain he or she is not moving a pendulum or planchette, and yet still direct small movements that are exaggerated by the device. In order for a planchette to be any good, it should be able to slide freely on the Ouija board, so that very tiny movements produced by the ideomotor effect can snowball into a motion large enough to highlight a letter or number.

The only way to rid the Ouija board of the ideomotor effect would be to blindfold the participants and occasionally rotate the board so they are unaware of the location of the letters and symbols present. Try the test yourself. Some Ouija board believers actually prefer to use the Ouija board without looking, and to have a nonparticipating bystander simply take notes on what the planchette spells out. Other Ouija board believers think the board has to be used with eyes open to work, because the spirits channeled use the eyes of the players to see the letters they want to select. If that's the case, there is no way to control for the ideomotor effect.

three

The Ouija Board's Reputation

I still remember the television commercials for the Ouija board when I was a kid. Children were playing with the board with both hands on the planchette. One kid would shout with wide eyes, "You're moving it!" The other playmate would deny vehemently, "No, *you're* moving it!" Throughout my childhood and young adult life, the Ouija board sat on game shelves, right next to Monopoly, chess, dominoes, and playing cards. Made of brown and tan cardboard and wrapped in plastic like any other game, the makers employ a marketing department that invents slogans like "It's just a game, isn't it?" Even the planchette is made of plastic that can easily be stepped on and broken. Don't worry, though, another Ouija board can be picked up at your local toy store.

At the time of this writing, Hasbro no longer sells the familiar brown Ouija board, but a new incarnation is available. The latest board, "The Mysterious, Mystifying Game," is now black and white in a blue and purple box. Both the planchette and the board glow in the dark, leaving the nonglowing letters and numbers in sharp contrast. The Parker Brothers logo appears on all sides of the box. On the one hand, a glowing Ouija board is practical. Pure genius, it would seem, since most sittings with the channeling tool may be performed at night or by the glow of candlelight. On the other hand, the glow-in-the-dark version of the cardboard contraption seems to scream novelty, now that it no longer wears the brown and tan coloring that simulated aged wood and gave it an air of antiquity.

There are those who believe this board should not be sold to children. There are those who believe it should not be distributed at all. Driven mostly by religious beliefs, but also by a secular desire to thwart scammers, Ouija boards can be viewed as tools created to deceive people. As a result, there is controversy wherever Ouija boards are sold, as individuals or groups of people fight to keep their children from making a purchase, or try to keep the board out of the inventory entirely. At this time, the Ouija board is legal in all regions of America, even in locations where fortune-tellers and psychics are outlawed. It is quite the conundrum, since one valid use of the Ouija board is for fortune-telling and psychic mediumship. However, it can be used as merely a toy without attempting either.

Use of the Ouija Board in Popular Culture and Media

In movies, television shows, and books, the Ouija board is a common method of spirit communication, most often portrayed negatively as a door to evil. This won't be the only book that you find on the bookshelf with spooky stories that have to do with the Ouija board. In compilations of true ghost stories, there is almost always one that starts with two or more people and a Ouija board. After all, it is a widespread tool people use to contact the paranormal, so it is the most likely avenue for spirit contact for many people who would otherwise never be caught dead in a haunted house, so to speak.

On the fiction shelves, you'll find that the Ouija board often makes a guest appearance in series books that feature paranormal storylines and teenagers. Since most teens have either had an encounter with a Ouija board or at least know about them, authors can write an exaggerated fantasy that involves a Ouija board in order to make a scary story more relatable and plausible.

The Ouija Board and Religion: The Good, the Bad, and the Ugly

Two married Jehovah's Witnesses knocked on my door to share their ministry with me. Though they didn't want to be named in my book since they consider the Ouija board demonic, they recalled a terrifying story of when they used the Ouija board together as a young couple, and it had spelled out that the devil was behind the board. Though they were careful to explain that they don't speak for all Jehovah's Witnesses, they were adamant in their belief that no one should use the board, and even that it should not be sold, because they believe that it draws people away from God and closer to the devil. The worst case scenario might be a Ouija board user being possessed by demons, going insane, becoming brain damaged, or even committing suicide.

A friend of mine participated in a youth group at Second Baptist Church in Prescott, Texas, as a teenager, when she admitted to the group that she used the Ouija board. The leader, a reverend minister, told her that use of the Ouija board was not encouraged. He pointed out that other members of the congregation wouldn't approve as well. My friend didn't discontinue her use of the Ouija board at the time. In fact, her interest in the occult only intensified, and she progressed to trying other séance techniques and even trying to levitate objects with her mind. She told me that her congregation was always welcoming and loving, and never made her feel bad for her use of the Ouija board, despite their own spiritual objections to the practice itself.

When researching this book, I called several local Christian churches and asked if I could come and visit them to interview ministers about the Ouija board. All of the churches I contacted politely refused to make an appointment, so you can imagine how surprised I was to be handed a tract on the street that made specific reference to the O

I was attending a large and busy town
lady with a thick accent asked if I would
Jesus. She handed me a small packet of tr
ously purchased through a website that s
order tracts. They included a small bookle

John, a pamphlet on salvation, a leaflet of healing scriptures, and a prayer for protection.

In the protective prayer, the Ouija board was listed as a known way for any person to purposely or inadvertently give one's allegiance to Satan and hosts of wicked spirits. The tract advised that one who had used a Ouija board should speak a prayer aloud to name the Ouija board as a sin, and to verbally reclaim one's soul for Jesus. At the end of the tract, it suggested reading another tract about demonic possession. It would seem that the Ouija board is considered a portal for demonic possession by at least some Christians.

Religious objections to the Ouija board

In particular, some Christians believe the Bible is the only way God speaks. Since what is not of God is of the devil, believers who take the Bible literally think the Ouija board is thus demonic by the process of elimination. If you're not for God, then you're against him. Furthermore, the Bible states in Deuteronomy 18:10–12 the following:

> There should not be found in you... anyone who employs divination, a practitioner of magic or anyone who looks for omens or a sorcerer, or one who binds others with a spell or anyone who consults a spirit medium or a professional foreteller of events or anyone who inquires of the dead. For everybody doing these things is detestable to Jehovah.

Many Christians believe that, even though there were no Ouija boards when the Bible was written, the Bible is a document that is still valid today. The passage above, they believe, directly refers to the Ouija board since it is used for both divination and contacting the dead. For those reasons, the Ouija board is detestable under any circumstances, even as a game. Christians acknowledge that the Ouija board has the uncanny ability to be accurate in predictions of the future and knowledge of the past and present, and attribute that to the power of the devil.

It is said that the devil is behind the movement of the planchette on the Ouija board every time by every player, whether atheist, Christian, or anything in between. In the case where the Ouija board claims to be a deceased person, the Bible (Ecclesiastes 9:5) states, "As for the dead, they are conscious of nothing at all." The Bible states that deceased people are unaware of the world of the living, as they wait bound in a sort of sleep-like state for the return of Jesus, when they will be resurrected.

So if you can't get answers from God through the Ouija board, and you can't get answers from the dead, just who are these demonic forces according to Christians? The Bible says that God created all the spiritual beings called angels before he created humans. However, some of the angels turned away from God and initiated contact with humans in order to deceive them and challenge God's authority. Such fallen angels, rebelliously defying God to get to humans, are called demons in the Bible. Typically, demons work hard to lure people away from God and toward the devil's side. If they fail to do so, they attack and torment the people they have been trying to lead astray. So even a strong Christian who is confident that his or her prayers can ward away all demons should not use a Ouija board.

Sample Christian prayer to correct the sin of using a Ouija board

> *Heavenly Father, I must confess that I have used a demonic Ouija board that has drawn me away from your side and closer to Satan. I now renounce any allegiance that I have made to the devil and his hosts of evil spirits. I reaffirm my commitment to Jesus Christ as my savior and ask for your forgiveness. I swear to use the Bible as my guide whenever I am tempted by the Ouija board. In the name of the Father, the Son, and the Holy Ghost, amen.*

Some biblical scholars have different interpretations, however. I had the pleasure of interviewing David F. Dawes, an author and retired managing editor for the *British Columbia Christian News* in Langley, B. C. , Canada. Dawes worked for the Christian Info Society for fifteen years, and spends much of his free time researching controversial Christian topics for his own personal study. When I asked Dawes if he believed the logic that everything not of God as listed in the Bible is satanic, he replied, "That's a simplistic and dogmatic mindset, and faulty logic."

Dawes explained that, while he believes God does speak through the Bible, and especially through Jesus, he also speaks through the created world around us. Even the tools of divination can be used instead, as simple artistic prompts to spark creativity. Dawes did not think that anyone should be dissuaded from such a practice. The Ouija board, however, evoked only skepticism from Dawes. He thought that the Ouija board was a harmless game, and anyone believing they were talking to spirits or getting real answers were just fooling themselves. He did think, however, that this skeptical view should be talked over with children before they used the board, to allow them to come to their own decisions instead of being carried away with terror. After all, in Timothy 1:7 the Bible says, "God hath not given us the spirit of fear but of power."

The Christian God, Dawes expressed, is guided by mercy and would not hate or abandon to Satan those who use the Ouija board. Rather than being fooled by Satan, Dawes thinks that such gullible people are more likely fooling themselves with mere nonsense. Just because some magical divinatory practices are not what God wants to be practiced doesn't mean that a toy is a mystical tool of the damned. If somebody is silly enough to believe that the Ouija board is more than it is, it will be a trick of the mind, not of the devil. Pressing further, I asked Dawes what would be the worst that could happen, if the Ouija board were to be used as genuine divination.

He maintained that the tricks of Satan were usually done in combination with a person's own foolish mind tricks; more often the blame lies entirely in the person. Either way, the person can be drawn away from the true God and drawn toward the idea of using the Ouija board for evil uses, such as using it to acquire information for selfish ends or to harm others. Demonic possession is real and has been documented, Dawes added, but not in connection with the Ouija board. Those who use the Ouija board are just playing a game. At worst, Dawes thought it more likely that serious users are completely deluded on their own. While Satan may laugh, God would just shake his head gently and love them anyway. He told me about

Christians in New Mexico who burned Ouija boards in 2001, which he thought was just superstitious fear of a simple toy.

But what about biblical literalists who interpret that Ouija boards are bad? What do they believe should be done about Ouija boards? Firstly, they believe that nobody should ever use a Ouija board and that if one has used a Ouija board, one should repent in prayer for such a sin and ask for forgiveness, rededicating one's life to Jesus. Secondly, if one is in possession of a Ouija board or has access to one, it should be burned. In Acts 19:19, 20, the Bible saw costly books on magical arts destroyed. "Many of those who practiced magic brought their books together and began burning them in the sight of everyone." Finally, Ouija board access by others should be limited whenever possible by Christians. Individual Christians might do that by forbidding access to their children, by complaining to or boycotting stores that sell the Ouija board, and by seeking legislation against Ouija boards by writing politicians.

Currently there are some regional laws against fortune-telling, as well as others that have been removed since fortune-telling has been ruled a valid spiritual practice in some religious faith traditions. In strong contrast to the beliefs of biblical literalists, there are other faith traditions in which the Ouija board can take on a vital and even central role in practice and belief structure. In fact, the Ouija board may be one of a very few interfaith spiritual tools, because of its availability and secular use.

The Ouija board as part of a spiritual practice

The Ouija board has found its way into spiritual practices of those who honor ancestors or use divination as part of their practices. For example, many Neopagans use talking boards such as Ouija boards in the context of ritual worship. For these people, there are two times of the year when the veil that separates the world of the living from the world of the dead is thinnest; the first of May (Beltane), and the end of October (Samhain). In addition, every full moon is thought to be an especially good time to seek answers from divinatory sources. Consequently, every month there is an excellent opportunity to use the Ouija board for divination, while twice a year the Ouija board can be optimally used to contact ancestors. Pagans usually construct a visualized circle of power in order to allow the intentions of good spirits to be hugged close to the practitioners, while malicious spirits are kept at bay.

When used for spiritual purposes, some people choose to modify their Ouija boards, to buy spiritually themed talking boards decorated with religious symbols, or even to make their own. A Samhain ritual involving a makeshift talking board can be created with a piece of paper and a wine glass. Simply write letters, numbers, "yes," "no," and "goodbye" on a piece of paper, and then use an overturned wine glass as a planchette. The wine glass has a special symbolism to many Pagans, as the vessel represents the cauldron of the Goddess from which life springs and to which life returns. It also represents the ocean of emotions that one cannot cross with loved ones when they must pass through life and into death.

Some Pagans use the Ouija board to talk with entities other than spirits of the dead, such as elementals, fairies or even goddesses and gods themselves. Rather than paying a Spiritualist medium, Pagans are a "do-it-yourself" lot who tend to use Ouija boards solo or in a group worship context, sometimes making their own talking boards. As a result, they may be paradoxically less vulnerable to fraud even though they may have a greater belief in the power and versatility of the Ouija board.

Skeptics and the Practical
Controversy of the Ouija Board

Skeptics can hardly contain a smirk when playing with a Ouija board, considering it a boring child's game. Skeptics often point out that the Ouija board is not proof of life beyond the grave, and that anyone could be moving the planchette, subconsciously or otherwise. Some skeptics are more vehemently opposed to using the board, since harmless fun can easily become a cruel trick on the gullible.

How Your Friends Can
Influence You with the Ouija Board

Friends have an advantage over strangers in that they already know personal information about you. You might have shared something long ago that your friend can bring up at that moment to spook you. Since your friend already knows you, it can be considered "hot reading" instead of cold reading, since he or she is feeding you information that you both know is true. Your friend may not even intend to trick you. If the two of you are caught up in the moment and captivated by the Ouija board, it can be easy to ignore the more prosaic source of the information.

An established rapport—When you use a Ouija board with a friend, you already feel relaxed and comfortable. There's no pressure to perform, and you know that you are going to have a good time no matter what happens. Besides, you already trust a friend, and don't think that he or she would play a trick on you, especially about such a serious matter as life after death. If the tone of the Ouija board session suddenly turns somber, it may seem that a ghostly presence is the only explanation.

An excuse for failure—Chances are that you and your friends are not all expert Ouija board mediums, so you have a ready excuse if things get misinterpreted. After all, you know your best friends aren't perfect people, and you've probably seen them make everything from small to large mistakes before. If the Ouija board seems to say something completely off-base, it is easy to ignore when playing with friends. If a spirit doesn't even know how to spell his or her own name, you can chalk it up to your amateur efforts.

Cultural trend—Sharply observing popular culture, television shows, and trends in the culture at large can be a good way of predicting an individual's behavior. Even if you are pretty quirky and don't fit into a box, you are still a product of your generation and your culture. A stranger or especially a friend in your same demographic will certainly be attuned to what sort of things might be influencing you from the world at large.

Fifty-fifty predictions—You and your friend know that you will see each other again, which makes predictions rather nerve-wracking if they turn out to be wrong. With predictions that give a yes or no answer, or that have only two outcomes, you've got a pretty good chance at being right. For example, whether a job interview will be successful, whether a baby will turn out to be a boy or a girl, or whether a relationship will last. The ones that turn out to be wrong will simply be forgotten, or will be chalked up to the fallibility of two novice mediums playing with a simple board.

Greener grass—This technique capitalizes on the fact that we always wonder what would have happened if we had chosen a different path in life. The Ouija board can name an ex who was "the one that got away." For a person who chooses career over family, potential children can be brought up, while if a person stayed home with the kids, an old job can be named. What could have been is something that will always fascinate us. After all, everyone makes decisions that change life's course into different directions, and nobody is completely and perfectly content all the time.

Lucky guess—If you happen to have just lost somebody named "Jessie," the hit would be amazing. But you might stretch names to fit into your own ideas. "Jessie" could refer to a Jessica, Jess, or really any name that starts with a "J" if you are hopeful to connect with such a person. If you really don't know anyone whose name is even close, the miss can be glossed over and the two of you can move forward with the Ouija board session. Descriptive terms can be given as well that may be an easy hit, or can be ignored if enough of them match to be interesting. Throwing out age numbers and zodiac signs can be other common lucky guesses if they land a match.

Peter Pan—Predictions of this sort are where your partner at the Ouija board uses the planchette to tell you anything that you would like to hear. After all, we all hope that our loved ones are happy after they die and go to some sort of afterlife. This sort of thing might come through the board especially if you have unfinished business with a deceased person and are asking for forgiveness or resolution. Your friend knows you well enough to know what you want to hear most from the Ouija board.

Pollyanna pearls—Much like the Peter Pan prediction, this element of cold reading with the Ouija board involves happy outcomes. However, it necessarily starts with something that has been going poorly for you. Typically most people want their relationships and finances to be stronger. However, a friend might know some more about what parts of your life have gotten the most complaints out of you, and speak to that specifically.

Public predictions—If you make enough predictions about current events like airplane crashes and hurricanes, all the boring ones that don't come true will fall by the wayside, but you'll be really spooked when one does come true and remember it forever. Sometimes the problem may be of recall if your friend reads a news article similar to your prediction but can't remember the date given by the Ouija board. The two of you may collaboratively misremember the details of the reading.

Self-fulfilling predictions—These work pretty well among friends, because you know where each of you needs to improve, and these happy avenues for growth can be both remembered and checked after. If the Ouija board advises self-forgiveness and you start blaming yourself for something in the next few weeks, you and your friend will both be reminded of the Ouija board session, and you will work to change yourself. Self-improvement can be a big part of the Ouija board's advice.

Sherlock strategy—Friends who hang around you for a while can pick up on a lot of different clues about you and come up with a Ouija board recommendation that seems out of the blue—for example, that you should rededicate yourself to learning to play the guitar. Perhaps your friend knows that you used to have short fingernails on one hand from picking your guitar, but now she's noticed that the guitar case has just been laying around in your bedroom collecting dust, and that you haven't brought it up in conversation for a while. Those facts collect and can form a pretty good intuitive guess about what your past hopes and dreams have been as well as what your future wishes might be.

Stat fact—If you are in a specific area that has a high density of a certain type of person, your friend or even a stranger can posit a pretty good guess that you fit into the majority.

If most of your friends fit into a group of people, a Ouija board user can trick you by assuming that you also fit into this category. Think about ways your gender, race, or region can dictate your career path, preferences, and relationships.

Unknown fact—Your friend already knows whether you have a spouse, living parent, or other important person in your life. From there, it's quite easy to receive a faulty fact and turn it into an unknown to save the Ouija board's credibility. After all, if something isn't going on in your life, your friend can easily say that the answer you receive applies to your household but it is something your significant other would know that you might not. For example, if an unfamiliar name is given, it could easily be assumed to be a friend or coworker of a friend.

How Complete Strangers and Scammers Can Influence You with the Ouija Board

A talented person can influence you without knowing anything about you. It doesn't matter how intelligent you are—you can still be fooled if you are in the right headspace to believe what the other person is saying. In most games with the Ouija board, it can be harmless fun, but it can also be used for fraud. Remember that a friend or relative would have an even easier time influencing you as a practical joke, since they could also rely on the techniques above.

Asking about experience with the Ouija board—It would be very embarrassing for the Ouija board con artist to have a Ouija board giving conflicting advice from a previous Ouija board session. Thus, an experienced person will probably ask you if you have used a Ouija board before. You might open up and unwittingly give some clues as to how this reading will proceed.

Credentials—A complete stranger with credentials, such as generations of experience or fancy certifications, is more credible than one without, plain and simple. If somebody is seen to have experience or qualifications, or both, you can feel more relaxed since it would seem that you are in good hands. Any fears or worries that nobody knows what will happen next are allayed, because you're just one more person in a long line of satisfied customers.

Establishing a belief system—If you don't know anything about the Ouija board, you'll be less likely to believe that it works. If somebody sets the stage for you and makes its origins seem a little more mystical, you can find yourself intrigued. Perhaps it will be claimed that the Ouija board was passed down from a family of witches or magicians. A stranger might also share a little bit about his or her belief in the afterlife in order to get you thinking about the reality of spirits contacting you from beyond the grave. If you're with a genuine believer, it will feel less likely that he or she will purposely try to trick you or play a mean game.

Fear elimination and setting you at ease—It is in a stranger's best interest to seem innocuous to get you to let down your guard. If you are concerned about your safety or well-being, you will not be open to the experience and will not easily be fooled by what anyone has to say. But if you feel like the Ouija board is completely harmless, you're more likely to relax into having a good time playing a game. Maybe the spirit guides will be given silly names and only give positive advice in order to make the scenario seem disarming and relaxing.

Barnum statements—Named after con man P. T. Barnum, these statements apply to just about everyone reasonably well, such as that everyone wants more respect and money, and has high hopes and dreams. Tying Barnum statements together during a Ouija board session can produce a rather vague and imprecise set of answers about personality and life in general, but they will be accurate for the vast majority of people.

Factual predictions—These predictions have a pretty precise time frame, but they are forgettable if they don't come true—for example, the prediction of a wedding in May or travel in September. If you were to have one of the events in a factual prediction happen, however, you might be fuzzy on remembering the time frame. If both elements of the prediction are correct and remembered, then it is something that you will tell your friends and family about for years to come. Factual predictions are pretty easy to make with the Ouija board, and are a low-risk strategy for a Ouija board partner to use.

Certain predictions—If the Ouija board doesn't predict a time frame in which things are going to happen, there are plenty of predictions that can be sure things. After all, we are each going to meet new people, get phone calls from people we haven't heard from in a while, experience buyer's remorse, and experience a few bumps in the road with regards to our health and well-being. The trick is that these predictions might be just around the corner or years down the road, and without context, they are pretty meaningless.

Likely predictions—Unlike certain predictions, these are given some fairly specific time frames. However, they are still pretty likely to happen. The events themselves are often left vague, so as to be open to interpretation. Accordingly, the Ouija board may just spell out one word like "accident" instead of an entire more specific sentence like "falling off a ladder." An accident can also mean a physical one like a car wreck or a cut with a knife, or a simple mistake you need to correct.

Unlikely predictions—These are actually supposed to be false, but incredibly specific. For example, the Ouija board could predict you will sing on a stage within the next two months, or be in a car crash in the next six. The Ouija board partner is counting on the fact that the two of you probably won't see each other again, so these mistakes will be discounted. However, if one of them does come true, you will end up becoming a true believer. Your Ouija board partner might even alert the media and become rich and famous over such a lucky strike, so it is worth making these unlikely predictions every once in a while.

Childhood memory—Some pretty predictable events happen to all of us when we are kids. Children get sick and injured, teenagers explore artistic and other talents that are later abandoned, and our first lucky breaks at landing jobs usually have more to do with who we knew or with being in the right place at the right time. If the Ouija board lands on any of those themes, it can seem to have tapped into your past in a weirdly accurate way, while actually expressing some common experiences.

Forgotten memory—Childhood memories are fertile ground for somebody to trick you. Not only can they use a spirit that was active when you were young, but they can also rely on the natural amnesia that happens for people up to the age of three. For example, the Ouija board could give a message about a rather nasty burn in a fire you once received. If you don't remember the occasion, it can be explained away by the idea that it happened when you were little, and you just don't remember now. Anything you do remember will seem like an amazing hit for the Ouija board, while anything that you don't think happened can be chalked up to faulty memory.

Direct questions—The best technique for getting information out of you is simply to ask you directly. For example, "There is somebody very specific you want to contact through the Ouija board today. Who is that?" A direct question is also difficult to directly dodge without seeming incredibly rude. Of course, there are many clever ways to accomplish this that make it seem like the person on the other side of the Ouija board either already knows, or is genuinely curious from the impressions that he or she is getting from the board. A startling question might be, "What is it about your health that concerns you so much?"

Diverted question—With any topic, such as career or love, the Ouija board might bring up the topic itself as a word without offering an entire sentence, since that involves considerable planchette movement. Your partner at the Ouija board can use this opportunity to ask some pointed questions that can subtly divert the reading without your awareness. If you answer in the negative, it means that the direction of the reading has to shift dramatically. For example, if the Ouija board were to spell out "unwell," you would be directly asked what you thought that meant. The word could be interpreted as either a physical illness or a state of emotional unease depending on how you react or help to interpret the word.

Embarrassing fact—An example of an embarrassing fact that somebody might take to his or her grave would be something like cheating on a spouse. A family secret, like a legal problem or a relationship taboo, is a perfect fact for a Ouija board trick. You will have no way to verify the fact, since the person in question is dead and all other people in your family either won't know about it or would naturally be keeping the secret as well. These tricks can add a little spice to any Ouija board session without compromising its credibility.

Emotionally correct—A wrong answer can be instantly turned symbolic by a clever Ouija board trickster. When a fact is a mere symbol, it can be interpreted along a spectrum of literal or figurative truth until it hits home. If it was right the first time, it will seem like an amazing hit, but there is no risk if any statement can be made into a metaphor. For example, the Ouija board could claim that somebody had a son. If the child was a daughter, it could be argued that the person always wanted a son, but the dream was never realized, and so perhaps a daughter was turned into a tomboy through upbringing. It could also refer to a boy treated "like a son," perhaps in a mentoring setting.

Fine flattery—Too much flattery may be obvious to you, but there are some things that work on nearly everyone, like complimenting caring, thoughtfulness, hard work, independence, and intelligence. For example, everyone tends to think that they are more honest than the average person. Even somebody who has to tell the occasional lie for safety or to preserve somebody's feelings probably considers themselves a fairly honest person at heart. Flattering intuition or open-mindedness can also help the stranger increase your investment in the Ouija board session.

Folk wisdom—Rome wasn't built in a day. Too many cooks spoil the broth. All those cliché phrases are famous for a reason. Folk wisdom is not only appealing, but it applies to everyone because it speaks to the common experiences of the human condition. Chances are that familiar phrases will also be those that you are most likely to remember as well as those with which you are most likely to identify.

Either way, a Ouija board partner has nothing to lose by repeating them during a session.

Forking—Like a diverted question except not requiring a question, this technique, often combined with a Barnum statement, allows the person interpreting the Ouija board to either expand on a topic or to backpedal, depending on how the person being tricked reacts. If the person agrees, it is safe to enthusiastically embellish the personality trait being highlighted. If the person disagrees, one can simply paint it as a lesson learned in the past. For example, one could safely accuse a person of being shallow, as spelled out by the Ouija board, but if there is a strong negative reaction to the statement, it could be brushed away as something you have worked hard to overcome.

Future right—The time scale can easily be slid to a future prediction to avoid a missed fact. It will seem like an amazing hit if the Ouija board lands on a unique name of somebody special in your life, but if that name means nothing to you, your Ouija board partner can just slide the time scale. Things in the future can't be verified yet, and if your partner gives you no particular time frame, it can never be proved wrong. This works especially for names that are not immediately recognized.

Fuzzy fact—Whether your great-grandmother died of lung cancer, heart disease, or even a car accident, pointing to the chest area as a cause of death is a pretty good cold reading technique. After all, everyone dies when their lungs stop breathing and their heart stops beating. Another example would be a mention of somebody in your life who wears a uniform—it could be military, police, or many service jobs, and it is very likely you would know at least one person who wears a uniform. Being vague about the specifics can allow you to feel like the Ouija board partner knows a lot more than he or she does. In actuality, you are filling in the gaps.

Good-chance guess—This strategy uses probability that may not be common knowledge. For example, the guess that there is a number two in the address of your home or workplace is a good one. It is actually incredibly likely that you have a low number somewhere in any house number, as is the likelihood that you have a popular color of car. However, the statements are so precise that they may seem shocking even when they are not.

Indirect questions—"Has this Ouija board session been making sense to you so far?" "Can you see why this is the impression that I am getting from the message?" "That last word was significant to your life, wasn't it?" Indirect questions can be peppered liberally throughout the Ouija board session without you even knowing that they are there. They pose as simple clarifying questions, ostensibly to make sure you aren't being left behind due to a confusion of vocabulary or intent. But actually, such questions can be a major force in directing the flow of how the Ouija board session will go. There are numerous ways to use indirect questions to make it seem like your partner is just collaborating with you and not leading you.

Jargon blitz—Ouija board users may use some pretty specialized language that fits into belief systems with which you may not be familiar at all. The words from astrology or specific religious traditions may seem to make sense in context, or you may have to just make up meaning as the session goes along, trying to get the gist of what is being said. Regardless, using a lot of jargon is a great technique your Ouija board partner can use to make it seem like information is flowing when he or she is actually asking you a question to get the session back on track. If you don't know what your partner is saying, you might tell them what they want to hear.

Psychic credit—It could easily be claimed that you are intuitive or psychic yourself, and you might very likely take that as a true message from the Ouija board. Those who are willing to try out the Ouija board are probably more likely to believe in the existence of psychic mediumship ability, and are thus more likely to consider themselves to have it. Attributing a positive psychic credit is one way that a stranger can convince you to take the Ouija board seriously. After all, by discrediting its messages you'd be discrediting something special about yourself.

Push statement—This statement is actually meant to be a miss, at least in the immediate moment. For example, an elaborate story about there being a time when you were waiting in a very strange chair for somebody important would be a push statement. Usually way off-base, a push statement is intended to prove that your Ouija board partner discovered something you didn't even remember yourself. It is incidental but very specific, and designed to have you immediately scratching your head. After a while, though, there is a good chance that you will think up a correct match for the experience. When that happens, you will be completely amazed at the oddly specific details.

Rainbow ruse—A clever Ouija board user can nail your personality traits without even knowing you by saying that you are two opposite things. That may seem counterintuitive, but it means that you can fall anywhere along a spectrum of human characteristics that describe everyone. You can be either extreme and still hear the right thing when the Ouija board gives you a rainbow ruse. A good example of a rainbow ruse would be for the Ouija board to say that you are both shy and friendly, perhaps quiet when you first meet people but more boisterous around friends. Another good rainbow ruse is to claim that somebody is both orderly and chaotic in different contexts, such as having a messy living room at home but a very structured office environment.

Seasonal element—There are some pretty predictable cycles related to the seasons. If it is the spring, the Ouija board could mention spring cleaning and probably be spot on. If it is the middle of the summer, the Ouija board could mention shopping or sales and probably land on some of the activities that happen to be at the forefront of your mind in everyday life. And of course during winter holidays, people don't want to be alone and are spending plenty of money on gifts.

Sugar lumps—In order to get you to believe something to which you wouldn't ordinarily give credence, some confidence artists will deliver complimentary rewards for keeping an open mind. Sugar lumps make sure to praise receptivity to the belief systems that would allow you to think there really is something magical going on with the Ouija board. The convention is that men can be fooled by stroking their egos. Their acute perceptions are what help them to succeed in business and attract women. Women may be credited with "a woman's intuition" and given anecdotes about anticipating children's needs or the arrival of important visitors. Anyone can be told that the Ouija board session is more powerful than any ever experienced before, and that blessings can be received if one is open to the extreme energy.

Nobody knows—Health problems can be claimed pretty liberally as the cause of death for spirits that come through the Ouija board, especially if the spirits are long passed and their health situation in life was unknown. Even if somebody died due to suicide, homicide, or accident, nobody knows what other health problems may have been present at the time of death. For example, the Ouija board could say that there was cancer in a person who died in a car accident. It may seem like the answer was wrong as a cause of death, but who knows whether the person had undiscovered disease at the time of the wreck?

Picking common themes—There are four pretty common things that just about everyone asks about when they think that the Ouija board can answer questions truthfully: love, career, money, and health. By hitting these topics, it will seem like the Ouija board knows your deepest concerns. There are a few minor themes as well that can always bring interest over the Ouija board, and those are predictions about travel, education, or other ambitious dreams or goals. Of course, travel can be interpreted to be anything from a spiritual journey to a business trip. If you aren't careful, you might just end up filling in the blanks yourself.

Jacques statement—"Have you changed from when you were younger? You used to have so many passions and dreams, but a lot of them had to fall by the wayside for practical reasons. After all, you had to get busy making a way for yourself in the world. Now you need to work harder to carve out space to have some spiritual or creative moments in your life. You've found yourself stuck in a rut and it is time to climb out." Okay, so that example might only work if you happen to be past a certain age. The point of the Jacques statement is that people go through similar struggles at specific points in life. By focusing on predictable crises in life, these statements can seem more profound when put in the context of a session with the Ouija board.

Russian doll—This technique can start out with something specific that can be wrong, but could be interpreted in many different ways, some that are quite a stretch. If you don't have a son, the message could be interpreted to be any young male in your life over whom you have some influence. Another good example is if the Ouija board were to spell out "music" and your partner asked you what role music played in your life. That could be playing an instrument in the present or past, or simply having meaningful music to listen to, something nearly universal. Spelling out "collection" is another good one, since many of us have a collection of some sort.

Trivia fact—If you're female, you probably used to wear your hair longer as a child than you do now. If the Ouija board told you that, you might be amazed. Trivia facts are actually just common knowledge, but it always feels like we're more unique than we are. Chances are that we've kept things like calendars that are out of date or old drawers that don't work quite like they're supposed to and hobbies that have been long abandoned in our homes, but when they're named specifically it can seem startlingly precise. Other things most people have are old photographs stored in a box, jewelry, a broken clock, a key that doesn't really go to anything anymore, and so on.

Unverifiable prediction—Do you have a secret admirer who will never be brave enough to ask you out? The Ouija board can never be wrong if it makes predictions that can never be verified. These sorts of predictions can be exciting and appealing to the people using the Ouija board, but of course they can never be either proved or disproved. Too many of these predictions would be obvious, but if your Ouija board partner is cunning, he or she will slip in one or two to fool you.

Unimportant mistake—Once the Ouija board lands on something correct, your Ouija board partner gets a free pass to make a few trivial mistakes without you becoming too concerned. Dates and hair and eye color can fly right past you without being a big deal if they are off. Wouldn't a dead person communicating through a Ouija board not care about how they looked in life anyway? You're likely so excited about the correct bit of information that you are willing to let it slide if other things are wrong. Besides, it's reasonable to assume that things like time and appearance might not really be the same for a spirit.

Persistence—The Ouija board pushing the issue of a wrong name may seem odd. It might seem like it is a good idea to backpedal every time there is a wrong answer, but skilled or talented cold readers may be downright insistent about some claims. By persisting, the Ouija board partner can get you to rack your brain until you fill in the blank. It makes your Ouija board partner seem honest and committed to figuring out the puzzle of the Ouija board with you. Who knows, you might just come up with a match for the name in your life when the Ouija board session is over, having forgotten that it was supposed to be a dead person.

One-way verifiable prediction—These types of predictions will only be proven to be true if they come true, but they can never be proven false. They are a sort of safety net for a Ouija board partner who wants to get the credit if an amazing thing comes true, but who doesn't want to have to worry about you thinking that his or her Ouija board use is fraudulent if it doesn't come true at all. For example, the Ouija board could tell you that a friend is taking a pregnancy test and worried about the results, but since you would only find out if it were positive, then the prediction could be right either way.

Vague predictions—Predictions about a journey, something new coming into your life, significant events, or anything else left vague, are very powerful during Ouija board sessions. They trick your mind into filling in the blanks. For example, a new door opening in your life could be a new job, a new relationship, or just a fresh outlook on life. The more symbolic the words seem, such as turning over a new leaf or getting stuck in a rut, the more vague the prediction may actually be.

Vanishing negative—"You don't want to have children, do you?" If the message coming from the Ouija board comes out of the blue and is asked about quizzically enough, it seems like an honest question about the interpretation, and not a subtle attempt to fool you. If you answer in the affirmative, the reading can continue on about the children you are likely to have and make the decision not to have children seem like a silly one. But if you answer in the negative, your partner can simply say, "No, I didn't think so" and then easily move on to other goals in life while still being perceived as correct. The scammer might even gently put down the option of parenting, making that seem like the ridiculous option. The vanishing negative is a way to ask any question that can seem like either answer is the one that your Ouija board partner was expecting.

Veiled question—The questions start off with a lead, to be sure, but they are still just questions. If you say no, your Ouija board partner can easily apply them to something completely different without having you suspect that the Ouija board might be entirely wrong. For example, the

Ouija board could spell out Jim, and then you could be asked whether there is anyone in your life who goes by Jim, Jimmy, or even James. You'll end up pondering the connections yourself and doing all the work to make the Ouija board make sense. Common themes like names, travel, and money can apply to various aspects of your life in different proportions and ways. By watching you and varying between using a tone that makes a statement or asks a question, somebody can fool you into thinking that you are getting information instead of giving it. Chances are that you will fill in the banks for the Ouija board partner.

What Scammers Can Do with the Ouija Board Once They've Influenced Your Beliefs

There are many skeptics who would contend that all encounters with the Ouija board claiming to contact anyone or anything are scams. During the time of the Spiritualist movement when Ouija boards were experiencing a rise in popularity, there were many Spiritualist mediums who used the Ouija board and other techniques to fool people. These people may have paid money for a sitting or may have increased the fortunes of the mediums by spreading the word about their mystical powers.

For example, other phenomena were often added when channeling with tools such as the Ouija boards. One of these was rapping. When asking a question of the spirits, instead of asking the Ouija board to indicate with a yes or no, the medium would ask the spirits to make a knocking sound somewhere in the building, two for yes and one for no. The rapping noises would add to the mystery of the Ouija board, since clients could clearly see that the medium's hands were still on the board, and unable to knock on the table or walls. Of course when the scam is later revealed, it would transpire that the knocking had been produced by accomplices hidden in an adjacent room.

An even more elaborate fraud was often performed involving table tipping. The table at which the people were seated would move around violently, seemingly of its own volition. You can imagine that, when combined with a Ouija board, believers would be suitably terrified by the ability of the spirits not only to move the planchette, but the board and table itself. Though a skilled medium could use slight-of-hand to move the table with his or her knees or foot, most often table tipping was performed by a rigged table that could be moved by a special mechanism, or by helpers hiding below the floor.

Although not all mediums who employed table tipping and rapping were unmasked as frauds in their day, it speaks volumes that neither practice has survived to this day. However, one friend of mine did notice that when using his grandmother's Ouija board in the attic of an old farm house, he did hear creaking noises. Another friend remembered trying to sleep in spite of the sound of footsteps creeping up and down the hallway floorboards. This would always happen the night after using a Ouija board. Certainly, if these are valid experiences, the phenomenon of rapping could rise again someday if sincere practitioners requested such activities from the spirits.

Stories of people robbed due to fraudulent mediums

Sadly, fraudulent mediums of all types still exist today, and are not just limited to mediums who charge for seats at a séance and then produce table tipping, rapping, or bogus messages from a Ouija board. Many more modern frauds will prey upon individuals who, while wracked with grief, approach them to try to contact dead relatives in order to find some closure.

In one case, seventy-one-year-old Clara Hoover was fooled out of $59,285 by a medium named Margaret Faulkner, a woman in her fifties. Clara had consulted the Ouija board many times, and believed it to have supernatural powers. With Margaret, the Ouija board began requesting jewelry and cash for "the good angel." The Ouija board instructed Clara to give the money and jewels to a gypsy named Yuma in a church. Clara did as she was told. But later, when she came to her senses, she took Margaret to court in a civil suit. After forty minutes of deliberation, the jury came back with a ten to two verdict against Margaret. State Supreme Court Justice Jacob Markowitz said that he had never seen such a fraudulent case, and that the jury should have taken far less time to come to a conclusion.

Typically, a fraudulent medium will begin by requesting a reasonable fee for his or her time consulting with the client. The client gladly agrees and is happy to have somebody to listen to their tale of grief and woe. The session is usually found enjoyable by the satisfied client. At this point in the typical story, skeptics and believers may dispute what constitutes fraud. Believers may say that even mediums who go on to ask for more money may receive valid messages from beyond. Skeptics would say that no messages from the dead are genuine.

After the client is suitably convinced the relative has come back from the other side to give a message to the medium, the real robbery can begin. The fraudulent medium will give some sort of terrible and dire warning, usually that the client will die of a spiritual or physical affliction, or will have terrible luck in love. At this point, the medium will request a larger fee that would pay for a spell, cleansing ritual, or hex removal. The client, convinced of the medium's veracity, will gladly pay the larger sum of money. Follow-up sessions are often required, and more and more money will be requested until the client either runs out of money or begins to suspect that something is amiss. Unfortunately, the fraudster has usually made off with the money by then, especially if he or she claimed the money would be returned. The client is then left with little recourse other than to swallow their pride and contact the police.

Since I provide fortune-telling services to clients, I often receive clients who have already been the victims of fraudulent mediums. For example, one client of mine went to a medium and was completely convinced, at the time, that the medium had contacted her dead husband. But afterwards, she realized that it was easy for her to have been duped. While channeling, the medium told her that her husband died from something in the chest area, and waved his hand over the torso to indicate this. Immediately, my client was shocked and amazed that he knew how her husband died. He had been in a car crash and the steering wheel had impacted with his torso, immediately stopping his heart and lung function. Afterward, however, the client realized how vague the medium truly had been. Everybody's breathing and heart stops at death, and the torso could be involved in any number of fatalities, from a heart attack to cancer or any of the most common causes of death.

The medium had also told my client that she had a special piece of jewelry she still often wore, and that it was now okay to take it off. At the time, my client had cried with relief because she still wore her wedding ring. After discovering that she had been hoodwinked, however, my client came to realize that it is extremely common for women to seek out a medium while still wearing jewelry from the deceased, be it a grand-mother's pearls, a mother's locket, or even a father's watch.

Avoid Influence
When Using the Ouija Board

The most common reason adults avoid using the Ouija board is not because of religious objections or fear, but because of the simple fact that they don't want to be thought of as a fool. If you vow to yourself that you will not move the planchette no matter what, then logically it may seem that the person you are partnered with is playing a joke upon you. Any credence that you give to the Ouija board session then makes you seem like an idiot. That's no fun, especially if you want to be open-minded about things like the Ouija board. Luckily, there are some simple techniques you can use to block somebody's attempt at cold reading techniques to trick you. That way, you can easily let the planchette slide around at will and give what-ever answers are ready to come without opening yourself up to a practical joke.

Do not answer questions—If your partner at the board or even the Ouija board has questions for you, don't answer them, as they might lead the session and cause you to be the butt of your own joke. If your board partner has a question for you, you can politely ask that the question be saved for after the Ouija board session, so that it doesn't influence the messages that the Ouija board has for you. Keep your focus on the movement of the planchette and on allowing fascinating messages to come through, rather than taking breaks to talk and interpret in between each message.

Do not give feedback—Answering questions isn't the only way you provide feedback for the other person at the board to lead the session, although it is part of it. You might also be shaking your head or saying that something doesn't make sense. If you are asked if something makes sense, you can say that you don't know for sure and that you'll talk about it after the Ouija board session has finished. Keep a poker face and try not to let your expressions betray any emotional reaction.

Identify cold reading techniques—Familiarize yourself with the cold reading techniques included earlier in this chapter. Somebody who is playing a trick on you will likely use some of the techniques included, and you will be able to call them out on it right when they happen. For example, if you hear a Barnum statement, you can say, "Excuse me, but that could apply to anyone." If you hear a rainbow ruse, you can say, "Excuse me, but the Ouija board just told me that I was two different things. Which one is it?"

Keep calm—If you think somebody is playing a joke on you, you won't endear yourself to him or her or anyone else who may be watching by becoming hostile. Control your emotions and try not to be snarky or laugh at the Ouija board session. On the other hand, don't become weepy at sad news or the presence of a beloved deceased spirit at the Ouija board. Not only will keeping calm make jokes seem not very fun, but your demeanor will get more information out of the session if it does have some ring of truth to it.

Make an audio recording—Taking notes during a Ouija board reading is problematic because you have your hands on a planchette and the messages often come fast. Even with an impartial bystander writing notes, they may get all of the interesting or accurate predictions written while missing all of the obvious failures that mark the whole Ouija board session as a joke. If you make an audio recording of the Ouija board session yourself, you'll be able to listen to it after your reading to get your true impressions once you are not under the influence of the setting and the emotional highs and lows of the moment have passed.

Recognize and agree upon all questions—The instructions for the Ouija board state that everyone should agree on each question asked. This rule can also help you avoid letting a prankster lead the session. If you find your Ouija board partner asking clarifying questions or direct questions over the board to help him or her interpret the session, point out that he or she is asking another question and decide whether you want that question directed toward the board.

Above all, keep a good sense of humor. Remember that you are just playing a game, and sometimes laughing and a little give and take are part of playing a game with friends. If you are too defensive, you might stifle any chance for the Ouija board to give you startling and true information. Worst of all, if you are hostile or combative, you'll end up having a terrible time and making the whole situation not fun for any other participants as well. Keep a good natured, pleasant demeanor about the whole thing...but keep your wits about you.

The Ouija Board and Spirit Communication and Divination

Divination can be an amazing tool. It can help people confirm past events that may be confusing or mysterious. Divination can empower individuals with advice to change the course of their destinies. The power of divination can even help people discover the potential future paths that can be taken, in order to best decide what course of action is necessary. Traditionally, there have been many tools and techniques for divination, from palm reading to fortune-telling cards. However, the Ouija board has particular strength as a divination tool. The Ouija board is one of few divination methods that can spell out results in plain English, and that can be operated by a novice just as skillfully as by an expert.

As a tool for interacting with spirit guides or the higher self, the Ouija board can bring an inherently challenging practice within the reach of anyone. Other methods of communion with the higher self or spirit guides might take years to learn proper techniques. Some mediumship techniques require being born with, or subsequently developing, gifts, like being able to see spirits or hear messages. With the Ouija board, even those who don't usually hear or see anything supernatural can see messages right before their eyes. People who can't meditate to save their lives will be able to tune in with a Ouija board.

Novels and books channeled through the Ouija board

Pearl Curran channeled a spirit named Patience Worth through a Ouija board who enjoyed dictating novels, poetry, short stories, and even plays. From 1913 to 1918, Patience Worth supposedly wrote over four million words by spelling them out on a Ouija board. One such production was a three-hundred-thousand word historical novel called *The Sorry Tale,* about the life and times of Jesus Christ. Since Pearl Curran was a housewife who had dropped out of high school, it was thought that she couldn't have been such a prolific writer on her own and that she truly must have received spiritual aid.

Pearl Curran wasn't the only one to write a book that was at least inspired by a session with a Ouija board. In the 1920s, books dictated through a Ouija board became a fad. Emily Grant Hutchings went so far as to say that her novel, *Jap Herron,* was written by Mark Twain from beyond the grave through a Ouija board.

Some of the literary works channeled through Ouija boards were quite good. James Merrill wrote *The Changing Light at Sandovar* during séances, and it went on to win the National Book Critics Circle Award. A piece from that work was included in a compilation that won the Pulitzer Prize for poetry. Another channeled work of his, *Mirabell: Books of Number,* won the National Book Award for poetry.

My First Ouija Board
Book Writing Experiment

As I sat here writing a book about the Ouija board, I thought to myself, "Why shouldn't I get in on the fun? If it helps my book, so much the better." Since playing with a Ouija board alone and writing the results in this book was something I could easily accomplish, I decided to experiment by trying solitary Ouija board use with and without the trappings of sacred rituals. Personally, I'd characterize myself as not inhabiting either end of the spectrum that ranges from skeptic to believer. I sit somewhere in the middle and try to keep an open mind. Perhaps you could call me a "critical thinking believer" or a "gullible skeptic."

So first, I stripped away all of the things that might tempt me to imagine the board to possess special properties and simply asked it if a spirit was present. The planchette slid immediately to indicate "yes." I wasn't surprised. I told myself that I was probably more prone to the ideomotor effect than your average person, since I have shaky hands, an impatient mind trained by video games, and the impulse to complete every sentence I hear. I asked if I could call forth the spirit of William Fuld, and the board indicated "no." Again, no surprise there, given my personal bias. I asked the name of the spirit, which simply echoed my thought, "Spirit." So I asked the spirit to write me a poem. I am terrible at poetry, and I thought this would be a good indicator of writing style. This is what resulted:

> *Have light own your eyes.*
> *Your hand is forced enough.*
> *Release your thought grip on the undone.*
> *Jokes are the mind's recess.*
> *Don't get lost.*

No rhyme structure, not even a haiku. I note that it is better than my usual terrible poetry, with forced rhyme and a tendency for contrived vocabulary and faux-archaic syntax, but it's certainly not great. Considering the time it took me to produce such a short message (about half an hour), I gained a fresh appreciation for those who wrote epic novels with the Ouija board. I thought that this might still be a fun project, but only for someone with lots of time on their hands. Though the board did not yet go to "goodbye" on its own, I told myself I had more important things to do at that moment and ended my first Ouija board writing session.

For my next solo session, I had occasion to make the timing just right. I did not take the laptop in with me for fear of spoiling the mood, so the results are from memory (I recorded immediately afterward.) With candles lit, I began. The planchette seemed to fly for me this time, with only seven minutes passing from start to finish. I was only able to ask if a spirit was present and then ask the responding spirit a single question: "Dear Ouija. Of all the millions of homes that you've been in, what is the scariest story that you can recall in which you have played a part?" Here is the reply:

A girl had me write her suicide note. I made the wind howl and the windows shake. I made her paper fly. She didn't care. She didn't listen until the end. She didn't care. I entered her mind and she cried out in my voice. I regret that we destroyed her. Goodbye.

I would have liked to have had more from my second session, especially as it went so fast. But I felt the need to respect the "goodbye" the planchette landed upon with such purpose. I feel that the second session had the flow that could allow somebody to write an entire novel using the Ouija board, although of course it would have to be broken up into many sessions in order to allow for rest and for each message to be jotted down from memory with accuracy. Readers, keep an eye out for an upcoming novel written by my Ouija board and me.

The Ouija Board as a Common First Exposure to the Paranormal

My best friend's dad, a Lutheran, told my friend that my Ouija board wasn't allowed in their house. He was an unusual guy, though, so to this day we don't know if he forbade it because he thought it was a demonic portal, because he was just enforcing arbitrary rules, or if he was playing with our minds to make the spookiness of the Ouija board seem more intense. My other good friend during my adolescent years had Catholic parents who forbade the use of Ouija boards and even the Magic 8-Ball in their home due to religious prohibitions against divination.

When I was a child, I was allowed to play with the Ouija board all I wanted. I bought mine with my own allowance at a toy store where the brown cardboard box lay stacked among all the rest of the board games. My father was an atheist, who thought it was nothing but a game. My mother was, and still is, an open-minded and spiritual person who allowed me to explore the paranormal all I wished most of the time. She recalled having played with a Ouija board herself at a party when she was about ten years old. There were about five children attending the party, but only two at a time would use the

Ouija board. When her turn came, she paired up with another little girl who was obviously pushing the planchette. While all the other little girls excitedly asked for the ghost to spell its name, all my mom could think about was how stupid the whole exercise was since it was obviously her partner spelling the name. Before they finished their session, my mom threw up her hands and bowed out of the game, thinking it was too ridiculous.

Many years later, she let me play with the Ouija board as a kid, although she didn't join in herself. Then one day a superstitious friend of hers was shocked to find out that she had a Ouija board under her roof. My mother's friend was from the Philippines, and she believed in a vivid supernatural world. In it, there were spirits with which anyone could interact with ease. She thought that the Ouija board was a portal to an evil, more dangerous world. "You have got to get that thing out of the house," her friend said, with such conviction that it spooked my mother. The next weekend, she sold the Ouija board at a garage sale for two dollars, right under my nose. I was furious that it had been sold without my permission, never suspecting that my mom was purging her house of it, out of fear.

The newest board, shipped to me express overnight, says that it is for ages eight and up, so it most certainly is made for kids. A warning in all capital letters, though, reads "ADULT ASSEMBLY REQUIRED." In spite of the fact that there are no obvious choking hazards for younger siblings, and no pieces to assemble, the planchette could possibly be broken by a very determined toddler. At any rate, it seems to imply the need for parental permission, if not supervision.

An expert on Ouija boards and a collector of the boards themselves, Robert Murch, pointed out that Ouija boards are often a child's first paranormal experience here in America. At slumber parties all over the United States, in campground tents, on Halloween, and even in cemeteries and supposedly haunted houses, children are deciding whether there truly is life after death for the first time while using a Ouija board. So is it just a harmless toy whose significance depends upon the user's belief? Or is the Ouija board a gateway tool that leads children to more dangerous interactions with demons?

Toy Stores and Retail Sales Associates

My very first real job was as a retail sales associate for a game store at a mall when I was sixteen years old. We had very good training on how to deal with customers, whom we called "guests." We knew how best to help those who were dissatisfied with any of our games for any reason. Ouija boards weren't the only games in our store that were subject to the fears of our guests. Decks of tarot cards were also a source of public disapproval, as were our role-playing games that involved magic, mostly because at the time they were thought to be dangerously isolating for teenagers. Add to this the perceived danger of the magical and the demonic. Our guest services training instructed us to let angry customers vent their frustrations, and never to claim that we didn't have the power to do anything about it. "My manager isn't here today" is not what an angry customer wants to hear; instead we would say, "I am hearing that this game isn't right for you. Let's do an exchange."

One day, I was "facing" products, a boring task in which retail employees carefully make sure that the label of every box is showing properly on the shelf. Suddenly, an angry guest stormed in through the mall entrance. I greeted her cheerfully, but she was immediately combative. She informed me that her preteen daughter (who was not present at the time) had bought a Ouija board from my store, and this woman believed it to be an entirely inappropriate toy for a child. Puzzled because we didn't have Ouija boards in stock, I tried not to get derailed and followed my training to empathize with her. I asked her if she had the receipt and the game so that we could perform an exchange, but the woman wouldn't hear of it. "I don't have it anymore," she said haughtily, "we burned it. I'm just here to make sure you don't sell the device to any more kids."

At this point, I was in a pretty helpless position, since I certainly did not have the power to ban an item from inventory, so I tried to reassure her that we didn't have Ouija boards in stock because we were a small store and had to limit the number of products offered. Then I attempted to change the subject by offering to open and teach her any new game in the store of which she approved for her daughter. The conversation quickly degenerated when she insisted that not only were we currently selling the game, but that I had been the retail sales associate who had sold the Ouija board to her daughter. Not wanting to contradict a guest, I kept quiet eye contact and allowed her to tell me how angry she was—until she began to use some abusive language, at which point I requested that she leave the store. She stomped out with a flourish.

Recently, I went to several toy and game stores, as well as big box stores, in order to see who sold the Ouija board in my town and who did not. First, I went to several department stores to find that there were no Ouija boards on any of the shelves. Employees who had worked for years at department stores simply said they typically didn't sell Ouija boards and gave no particular reason, even though many other board games were present. When I went to a smaller specialty store, an employee said that, curiously, three other people had asked about the Ouija board in the past three months, but this store didn't sell games like that because they didn't want to compete with the larger stores' mass-marketed game sales. I was unable to uncover any sort of conspiracy against the Ouija board, but it is also unlikely that they have fallen completely out of favor.

Teachers

Years ago, I had the pleasure of being a middle school and high school science teacher for kids ages eleven through sixteen, the prime age group for Ouija board usage. Of course, we didn't have the opportunity to use a Ouija board in the classroom, although it would have been a fun prop for allowing kids to figure out how to format experiments or to demonstrate the ideomotor effect. You might think it odd to bring mysticism to school, but teachers are allowed to bring in all sorts of topics for discussion, and in fact when I returned to full-time fortune telling, I taught a class on numerology to elementary school kids through my local Chamber of Commerce Business and Education Exchange. The kids often spoke of the mysterious fun of Ouija boards, and even brought one along to eighth grade camp.

In general, the other teachers supported all manner of childhood explorations outside the classroom, but laughed and rolled their eyes at Ouija board adventures. Certainly, if a parent had raised objections about n Ouija board at school or on field trips, we would have had to respect that parent's beliefs. Typically permission slips were involved for controversial topics, and an alternative activity would have been provided for children whose parents didn't approve. Luckily for us in our district, most parents of eighth grade campers and hosts of the after-school antics of preteens and teens seemed to view the Ouija board as harmless fun.

At one point, a younger student came to me to ask if life existed after death, obviously assigning a great deal of assumed knowledge to my role as a science teacher. She told me that she had contacted her recently deceased grandmother through a Ouija board, and that the spirit on the board had answered questions that only her grandmother would have known. Of course, teachers must worry about the gray areas of life in which religious beliefs exist, so I did not want to overstep boundaries. I told her that nobody had conclusively proven whether there is life after death, and said that maybe someday she would be the scientist to design a proper experiment to gather evidence to answer such a deep question. Changing the topic somewhat, I asked whether she had spoken with her parents about her beliefs, and directed her to our school counselor for some much needed grief counseling.

In another case, an older student came to me because he had heard rumors that I was a Wiccan. The student told me he wanted to become a Wiccan too, but his parents disapproved of his religious choices and had taken away his Ouija board and tarot cards in order to limit his involvement with the occult. I empathized with his frustration at not being allowed freedom, but told him that his parents were responsible for his spiritual upbringing until he was an adult. I pointed out that he could probably earn more of their respect and trust by showing with his actions that he was still the same good and responsible person as he was before his interest in Ouija boards. Thus it would be wise for him to refrain from purchasing another Ouija board behind their backs. Instead, I suggested, he should work on improving his grades and fostering his community and family relationships, to prove how much his new spiritual interests were bettering him as a person. Mutual pride in his positive life changes hopefully allowed for a better dialogue between my student and his parents later on, but he graduated out of my class without speaking to me about it again.

Interestingly, when I approached several teachers, all friends, to interview for this book, they refused, even when I suggested using a pseudonym and not revealing their districts. Teaching is a very conservative environment, even in the liberal and secular region in which I live. If even one parent read the book and disapproved of a teacher who believed in spirits and the Ouija board, that parent could make a guess as to which teacher said what and cause trouble between the teacher and the administration. In a job where the contract is renewed each year, the job can simply be ended without cause or explanation.

Librarians

In my experience, librarians are champions of freedom of information, which extends to the use of occult literature available in the library and materials like the Ouija board. It was an elementary school librarian who invited me to teach the class on numerology through the Chamber of Commerce Business and Education Exchange, and who later proved to be a good sport about getting her own mediumship session to have a deceased relative channeled through me.

The Teen Librarian, overseeing several branches of the library in my county, holds a recurring summer teen mystical fair. During the fair, books on divination methods and paranormal phenomena that include talking boards like the Ouija board are spotlighted and I was hired to answer questions as an author and fortune-teller. On one morning before my first such appearance at the annual fair, I emerged from the shower to see my husband holding the phone and saying that the news was calling for me.

When I picked up the receiver, I discovered that I was being put live on the air on a conservative radio talk show, with a host that was positively livid that I would be exposing children to the occult at my local library. I probably wasn't at my most articulate in that moment, but I tried to explain my own beliefs that children should be allowed free access to information.

Of course, the library got wind of the controversy about the teen event. I apologized for any role that I played and offered to do the event for free, or to bow out, if they so chose. I imagined that there might be picketers and protesters present. The librarians gave me an amazing show of support, refusing to allow me to work for free and assuring me that they stood behind me completely. The day of the event arrived, and it went off without a hitch. A good time was had by all, and many children and parents attended, not only to pick up books on divination and ghostly phenomena, but to have me tell their fortunes. Happily, I was asked to return for future events by parents, children, and the librarian.

four

Spooky Experiences

The stories in this chapter are all based on real, true-life experiences people have had with Ouija boards. Certainly, such stories abound among teenagers in exaggerated form. As a kid, I remember friends claiming the planchette had flown across the room of its own accord. Of course, such fantastical stories fade over time when people realize that the imagination informs much of our memory. In the end, most are left with only the things that can be corroborated by other adult friends. Though memories are sometimes hazy about the exact details when recalling things that happened during childhood, I am surprised at how much the spooky details stood out for people who wanted to share their stories for this book. Other stories in this chapter are from more recent Ouija board parties held among adult acquaintances, very much like the Spiritualist dinner parties that were held when the Ouija board was first produced.

Inspiring Stories of People Connecting with Spirit Guides or Deceased Loved Ones

What follows are true stories that arose out of the use of the Ouija board, but they aren't necessarily the bone-chilling type involving spooky ghosts. Instead, the spirits who helped the people in these stories were well-meaning spirit guides or friends from the other side. Using the Ouija board doesn't have to inspire shivers or laughter; it can also bring tears of joy. The Ouija board has the potential to be a powerful divination tool, relaying messages from spirit guides, or even aiding the grieving process, allowing closure with deceased loved ones.

Accidental psychic detective

When I first started using the Ouija board, I ran into a problem that stayed with me when I began to try to speak to dead people through other means as well. To me, it seemed as if ghosts would seek me out in order to tell me messages that they wanted broadcast to the world. The first few times that I used the Ouija board as a young teenager, I seemed to get the same spirit over and over again. The same name came up when I asked what spirit was at the board, and I began to construct a belief system that perhaps only the ghosts immediately surrounding the Ouija board were able to gain its access. After only a few months of eager practice, I felt I was experienced with the Ouija board, but I was disappointed that I could only seem to contact a local ghost and not a spirit guide.

Many of my opinions would soon change. The first time I met a new ghost, I was entirely startled and wondered if somebody was newly dead in my neighborhood. I was seated in my childhood bedroom surrounded by flickering candles and a few good girlfriends who were eager to ask my familiar ghost some questions about boys. I was bored by those questions, being sort of a late bloomer myself. Turning my attention away from the Ouija board activities, I wandered around the room, lighting some incense to make the mood a bit more fun. Unexpectedly, one of my boy-crazy friends called my attention and said that there was a different ghost present, one of a young boy.

I cast a sidelong glance at my friend while poking the wax of a candle. I assumed it was an imaginary boy, to whom they would pose embarrassing questions for fun. "He's asking for you," my friend said. I sighed and dragged my feet as I went to the Ouija board. I loved playing with the board under most circumstances, but I was concerned that this particular group of friends was going to try to play a trick with a fictitious ghost who "had a crush" on me.

Many of us crowded around the board and were eager to learn what the ghost boy had to say. We squeezed shoulder to shoulder, each with one hand reaching for the planchette. "What do you want from me?" I asked. A part of me secretly hoped I was finally meeting a spirit guide. The planchette moved swiftly under our hands, with some girls losing contact and having to chase it around the board to rejoin the game. The first words were startling: "Help me."

In the dimly lit bedroom, sitting on a carpet, we watched the story of the ghost unfold on the Ouija board. The boy in the board was James, and he told us that he had traveled a long distance across the earth in order to see us, particularly me. I shifted uncomfortably in my chair. I had only shared with one friend that I thought I could see ghosts sometimes, and that friend wasn't present. I was worried that the rumor mill had spread my secret to these other friends. I looked in the eyes of the other Ouija board players to see if somebody was trying to get me to spill my guts. Instead, everyone looked at me enviously. I was the only one among my peers allowed to burn candles in my room and summon spirits through the Ouija board, and now I was a celebrity among ghosts.

James continued his message through the Ouija board, wanting to name the murderer who had started a fight and then ended his life. Another friend of mine at the board recognized the story. She said that her brother had witnessed a teenaged boy have his throat slit ear to ear. Another older friend of ours had been injured in the fight as well. Her brother wouldn't come forward with the truth about what happened, and he was damaged himself by the occurrence, currently spending his days and nights in a home for the mentally ill.

Several of us were beginning to become nervous. Even though I had an interest in the occult, I was a good kid, and had never been involved with anything as serious as murder or lethal violence. The thought that a ghost in the Ouija board was drawing me into his drama with the wrong crowd made me want to throw it in the trash. James told me he wanted his murderer brought to justice, and asked me to tell the police what happened. I shook my head and withdrew my hands from the planchette. The other girls looked at me expectantly.

"What?" I shrugged. "I'm not going to do it. If it was one of you moving that thing, then this information just isn't true." I said that I was pretty sure that giving false information to the police was a crime (it is) and I wasn't about to go to jail over a Ouija board. The room exploded with the chatter of each of my friends denying to all of the others that she was moving the planchette.

My mother burst into the room bringing snacks, a habit of hers whenever she overheard things that concerned her. Whenever she saw something she didn't like going on, she would putter about my room with the pretense of searching for dirty laundry. She took one look at the Ouija board and reached for her laundry basket. With the mood spoiled by the presence of a parent, the seemingly urgent Ouija board mission was abandoned.

That night, I told myself not to have nightmares. Over and over again I informed my brain that I did not want to see some boy stabbed to death. I went to sleep and got my wish. Instead, in my dream, I was the boy who was murdered. I saw his face in the mirror in a bathroom. I remember gathering details in my mind, making sure I would know the location and remember any names or faces that would be important to verifying the dream's truth. I recall being terrified when the dream took a darker turn toward the night of the murder, but telling myself that it was only a dream and that I was safe in my bed at home helped. As I was drawn into the story of the conflict, my rational mind left me, and I awoke drenched in sweat and flopping around as if I were kicking and fighting invisible enemies.

I knew I had to somehow get the message to the proper authorities without ending up in a jail cell. But the light of the dawning day made me doubt my dreams and wonder if it was just the night's excitement going to my head. I would have to consult with the other girls to see if they even still cared about our Ouija board session, or if it was forgotten as easily as some other quick thrill. My phone rang. Apparently my friends had already been working, after our Ouija board session, to figure out how to get the information to the police without getting in trouble. Luckily for us, my friend's uncle was involved in law enforcement, and he said he would gladly pass along the information. As I spoke with my friend, I took out a notebook and recorded some of the information from my dream in order to pass that along as well, feeling relieved that I wouldn't have to break any legal boundaries myself.

The next weekend, my friends again gathered at my home to call up the spirit of James, the ghost boy who had made us feel so important. I remember James spelling out "thank you" over and over, filling us all with a sense of pride. I felt like I had made a ghostly friend, and that instead of finding a spirit guide, I had been able to guide a spirit. At the end of that session, James wished us farewell in a way that seemed permanent. One of my friends announced that he had been allowed to pass over to heaven because of our activities. As an adult, my memories of the details are hazy, and I wonder if the uncle of my friend had just laughed at us and forgot about it. But I'll always recall the fond sense that my odd spiritual interests had helped somebody, if only on some other plane of existence.

Speak now or forever hold your peace

Steph used the Ouija board with her friend Tamera, excited to play and see what sorts of things might come through. Tamera wanted her friend to ask about her upcoming wedding plans. Steph in particular was a fan of fairies, and hoped that she would be able to speak with nature spirits or fae folk through the Ouija board. But, when Steph and Tamera first sat down to the board, their question "Is there a spirit here?" was answered with "goodbye." Puzzled, they asked whether the energy manning the board was fae or whether it lived in the house. The board went to the letters P and H.

Steph and Tamera thought about the letters eagerly, and searching their memory banks decided that it would be exciting if the "P" stood for the Greek goddess Persephone, and the "H" for her husband, Hades. Smiling, Steph asked, "Are you Persephone and Hades?" The planchette moved to "yes," and the two women were ecstatic.

Wanting to confirm her upcoming wedding plans, Steph asked the deities, "Should I get married in May?" The planchette quickly slid to "no." Steph looked shocked, but spoke aloud in a calm voice to herself. "Hmmm ... Well, I've got to do a lot of replanning. I already took the month off! Oh well, it's easy to replan. Should I get married later this year?" Thankfully, the planchette indicated the affirmative.

After a few times picking dates that were refused by the Ouija board, Steph decided to ask the board in which month she should be wed. The board pointed to the number 9, answering with the month of September, and Steph was able to convince it to agree with the answer of the Saturday closest to the equinox. She sighed. "Gotta tell David," she said, of her fiancé. At that point, the Ouija board started spelling what looked like gibberish. "Xealau ..." It slid past letters and pointed to the moon. "Maybe it's in Greek?" Tamera suggested. After all, they had been consulting Greek deities, and they could easily consult the Internet in the other room to have the word translated.

The two women decided the board had nothing more to tell them and ended the session. It was a first experience with the Ouija board for both of them, and had seemed pretty productive, indeed. When they later looked up the word that the Ouija board had spelled, it appeared that it hadn't been finished giving them a message at all. The Greek word was translated to "furthermore ..."

A businessman's question

Scott was an entrepreneur from out of town who came to a Ouija board party. He wasn't expecting to be there, but a friend he decided to meet up with while in the area wanted to offer him something unique to do, instead of the usual tourist traps. When he showed up, he characterized himself as a "believer." Scott was an older gentleman with gray hair and kind eyes. He practiced an indigenous spirituality he called "earth and sky," and was willing to use the Ouija board as a sort of spirit guide source. He had never used a Ouija board before, however, and was raised as a Catholic.

When Scott sat down at the Ouija board with another believing partner, she began the session by asking, "Is there a presence here?" The planchette immediately moved to "yes," and Scott could feel a mysterious and unearthly pushing sensation. He felt like he trusted the spirit guide enough to ask it an important question about his business. "Dear Ouija, do you like the idea of my solar marketing campaigns? Is it good for humanity?" Scott concentrated hard, willing to follow the advice of the spirit guide, while his partner at the planchette closed her eyes completely. "A lite eletik … us … you … " Both players thought that their hands felt tingly. The board continued, "plan each … " then the planchette jiggled between the letters "R" and "P." Scott smiled and murmured, "PR … public relations!" The planchette moved to "goodbye."

A grieving woman

Tonya was a skeptic who came to a gathering of friends after having lost just that week a very close loved one named Les. She and Les had a keychain that said "U. S." on it, but she didn't show it to anyone. She didn't tell anybody she met about the death, and took a chance on playing with a Ouija board with a friend of a friend that she didn't know. When the pair asked if a spirit was present, Tonya felt like there was a strange pulling sensation on the planchette.

Her skeptical partner remarked that she felt a heaviness pressing on her hand as the planchette spelled out "US." Tonya felt a chill, thinking about the keychain, but didn't talk about what she was thinking. Unfortunately, the board ceased to make sense after that point, spelling out "REF9" before saying goodbye. Strangely, Tonya felt she had seen the number 9 numerous times that week in a seemingly meaningful way. She decided to continue to think about the message and wondered if it was somehow from the person she lost in order to help her feel better about her grief process.

Months later, Tonya returned to the Ouija board, but was nervous about what message (or lack thereof) she might receive. She wasn't ready for closure, and was terrified that Les would not answer. She decided to show up at another party where a Ouija board was being used and select a stranger named Juli as a partner. Juli was reticent to be paired with such an obviously emotionally fragile partner, fearing that any lack of empathy skills or belief in the board on her part would harm Tonya.

When they sat at the board together, Tonya bravely forced herself to ask, "Les, are you with us now?" Nervously she giggled as she heard his voice ringing in her head. The planchette moved to "yes." Tears came to Tonya's eyes and she ended the session, not wanting to push her luck with the Ouija board. Juli grasped Tonya's hands. "See, you were brave and it paid off!" Tonya wiped her face and nodded before leaving the table and running from the room. That night, she kicked herself for not asking if Les had any message for her. Perhaps the closure wasn't a door closing after all.

In need of a guide

Donna went to a Ouija board party determined to make contact with some sort of guide who could help her through her life troubles. She felt like her life was a soap opera. Her ex-husband had recently been sent to prison for eight years for attempting to murder her. A new boyfriend had been shot in the abdomen in a fight, and she was working three jobs just to make ends meet for her and her two children. It was hard to get away from her troubles even for a night in with friends, so her mind was heavy with how to relieve some of the stress.

At the beginning of the evening, most of the party attendees were nervous about using the Ouija board, so Donna bravely grabbed her coworker Misty, who wasn't quite sure what this Ouija board thing was all about, to get the party started. As bold as she acted, Donna was still a little scared of using the board. She had heard a story about a woman who used the Ouija board at a party and had an evil spirit follow her home, so Donna hoped there were some sort of preventative measures in place.

After Donna and Misty centered themselves, they eagerly asked their questions. Donna wanted to know whether she would meet somebody new in the relationship department, and if so, what his name would be. Misty wanted to know if her deceased father, Francis, was present. Despite their hopeful attentions, the planchette remained still.

Misty and Donna wondered together whether there was enough energy in the board to get it going. They rubbed their hands together to form a ball of energy in their mind's eyes and then projected it into the planchette. Again, Misty asked if Francis was there, but the planchette remained still, seeming to be a clear negative.

Donna's mind, however, had wandered to other questions. She wondered if there was a spiritual presence in her house. She and others heard stomping upstairs when no other humans were present. Donna had dreams about speaking in tongues, which she believed to be associated with the strange thing in her house. "Is there anybody in my house?" Donna asked. "If so, what is their name?" The planchette finally grudgingly moved to indicate "M. V." and then the numbers 9 and 0. Donna said that the home was built in the 1990s.

The subject reminded Misty of her own encounters in her home. "Are the crosses on my door intentional?" Misty asked. The Ouija board indicated the affirmative. Misty explained that there were ten crosses marked upon her door. She also felt a presence in her home, and often felt like there was a spirit person crouching by the door upon which the crosses were marked. The Ouija board spelled out its name as "Ed C" before the planchette shot to the word "yes" again. At this point, Misty felt like she needed a break from the Ouija board, but Donna was still eager to learn more.

Donna grabbed another party attendee, named Stephanie, and got back to her original relationship question. "Am I going to meet a nice guy?" Donna asked. "Because the guy I'm with isn't nice to me." She explained the sad story about how her current boyfriend was cruel and angry, but that Donna wasn't sure whether it was due to his injuries or just the type of person he was. He was all apologies after a difficult encounter in their relationship, but Donna had the sneaking suspicion that she deserved better.

The planchette swept dramatically across many letters as it swirled in a counter-clockwise circle. "Wa lo.. fh … 5 … " Impatient with the board which didn't seem to know how to spell, Donna asked, "Do I know him? Have I met him yet?" The Ouija board indicated that she had not. Donna pressed for a date that they would meet, and the Ouija board indicated January 30 of that year, which was only ten days away! "What is the age of the man?" The Ouija board answered: "34 … no, 45." Donna's partner, Stephanie, laughingly asked, "Is he rich?" The planchette shot to "yes," and they giggled like schoolgirls.

They came up with more questions about the mysterious man Donna would meet, and they learned that he didn't have kids, and didn't want them. So, the women started narrowing down where they would meet. "Will they meet at the grocery store?" Stephanie asked. "No, jmp" the Ouija board said. They puzzled a bit over the letters given. "Is that a restaurant?" That's where the Ouija board seemed to take a silly turn. "Zoo" it spelled, simply. The ladies laughed tat the very idea, even when it indicated "yes" several times. The planchette circled the board nonsensically, spelling out gibberish. Stephanie joked about Donna meeting him by the penguins, two visitors together at the zoo on a weekday. It would be strange, indeed.

Shifting gears, Donna again pressed for the name of the spirit presence in her house. This time the Ouija board gave the letters N. Y. instead of M. V., but still insisted that they were initials. Still not frustrated by the illiterate spirit at the Ouija board, Donna asked, "Is he dangerous or hurtful?" Thankfully, the planchette indicated that no, there was no danger. By this time, Stephanie had gotten bored with the Ouija board's antics, so Donna switched partners again.

Going back to the subject of her current boyfriend, Terrence, Donna asked whether he was "going to get better mentally soon." The Ouija board sadly went to "no." Feeling upset, Donna asked if there was anything that he should focus upon. The board had trouble spelling the answer "acupu…" so it was suggested "acupuncture?" The guess was rewarded with a "yes." The board indicated stomach and spine issues, but again started spelling gibberish. "Es go…We lo ar." Donna's heart felt broken for Terrance. The energy around the board felt prickly and everyone in the room could feel Terrance's negativity.

Donna knew from the Ouija board that there was no love in her current relationship, but she just felt like there was too much commitment. She still wanted a definitive answer as to whether she should stick it out with Terrance. In addition to his attitude problems, he traveled away from her often, and she wasn't sure what would worry her most: If he left forever or if he asked to move in with her. The board tried to spell out that they should just be friends… "friean" it said. "So, help him out as a friend but not a lover?" The board indicated the affirmative, and confirmed that Terrance cared about her and wasn't a bad person. It reminded Donna of the other person on the horizon, and gave his name again spelled poorly. "Pffel" it said, which was taken to possibly be the name Phil.

With every ending, the Ouija board said there would be a new beginning. With poor spelling as always, it insisted the loss and fresh start was the "gygt" (gist) of the message for

Donna. Still seeking guidance about her family, Donna asked if problems with her fourteen-year-old son would end soon, but the Ouija board had bad news that no, they would not. Finally, wondering about the source of wisdom in her life, Donna asked the name of her spirit guide. The Ouija board was strangely confident as it spelled out: "Nipuaulu."

Dream big

Awen was having a series of difficult and dramatic life events when she decided to consult the Ouija board. Much like Donna, sometimes her life resembled a soap opera. She loved two men, both of whom were receiving treatment for cancer. She was trying to prepare a house for sale and, as many of us were in our troubled economy, attempting to find a stable source of income.

Awen consulted the Ouija board with her trusted friend Jian. Jian asked, "How is my brother?" The sound of the planchette scratching across the board filled the room, and yet it appeared to be stationary. Awen felt tension building in her hands. "R U?" the Ouija board replied. Confused, Awen asked, "What is your name, oh spirit?" The Ouija board's planchette moved agonizingly slowly, and the tension in Awen's arms built till it was too much to bear. She decided to take a break and puzzled over what was wrong. The board seemed to be very low on energy. Try as they might to rub their hands together to put energy into the planchette, it still moved quite slowly. Impatiently, they decided to try again in the morning when their own minds and bodies were fresh from sleep.

The next day, they sat back down at the Ouija board and Awen asked cautiously, "Can we talk to you?" The planchette moved smoothly to "yes," without any of the delay or frustration of the night before. "Who are you?" they asked eagerly. A name came through with insistence, even though it seemed that the spelling was unusual or possibly even backwards. "Eresfad." The board was just getting warmed up.

"Do you have any messages for us?" they asked. Charmingly, the answer was simply, "Dream big." Awen was shocked but inspired. In spite of her money woes and draining personal life, she had secret hopes of starting her own business. In disbelief she asked, "Will our dreams become manifest?" The board answered, "Of course." Now completely giddy with the idea, Awen continued with a more detailed question about the property she wanted to buy for her business. "Will we get the property across the street?" At the time of the Ouija board session, neither of them knew that the property in question had sadly already been sold to a different business owner. The Ouija board answered, "Establish service," seemingly directing her away from buying the unavailable property without crushing her excitement.

Puzzled, Awen asked, "What kind of service?" The Ouija board seemed to tease her for not knowing her own strengths, replying "Really?" After all, Awen was already a skilled cook who had been planning to make specialized treats as soon as she could get her hands on a commercial kitchen. This time, Jian was the one feeling the tension building in his arms, but to him it felt less like being tired, and more like the Ouija board's tingling flow of energy. It was exhausting. They decided to wrap up the session by asking if there was anything else that needed to be communicated at the time. The planchette drifted past the letters K, W, and J before shooting straight to "goodbye."

Awen was practically floating with joy as she got ready to start her day. One of the beloved men in her life was receiving an infusion of cancer treatment, but she was optimistic after her encounter with the spirit guide Eresfad. Jian went to get some fresh air and relax after the energetic experience. As he stepped outside, he noticed that an outdoor fireplace with a chimney had crumbled during the Ouija board session, right outside the room in which they had been using the board. He attributed the phenomenon to the powerful energy that had helped them jumpstart their day and their dreams.

My invisible friend

I've already told the story of the spirit I met when I was a teenager. Her name was Molly, and though I desperately wanted a spirit guide, I didn't feel she was one. For one thing, Molly seemed just as confused and bewildered about life and the world as I was. I was a nerdy kid who didn't have very many friends in school. In fact, I had purchased the Ouija board with money from my first job at a game store. Most of my gaming past times seemed rather immature and geeky to the other kids at school. Yet, any time I asked Molly for advice about making friends or avoiding enemies, she didn't seem to have a clue. She had gone to a one-room schoolhouse herself, and the social dynamic of a modern school system was something with which she simply had no experience.

Though I had given up on the idea of Molly as an omniscient spirit guide, I was never one to do the bare minimum when exploring the occult. I made my own Ouija board and had Molly help me calibrate it, asking her where she would prefer each letter to be located instead of simply listing the alphabet in order. I added extra words indicating moods on my Ouija board so I could easily find out how Molly was feeling and if she was up to answering a lot of questions or just wanted to be left alone. I went to the library and read books about ghosts, soon learning that ghosts could be kept inside an object called a fetter.

Since Molly was very lonely, I asked if she wanted to be placed voluntarily inside a fetter so she could come with me to school and see what it was like. Molly excitedly agreed to the idea. I didn't have access as a young teenager to very many impressive objects inside which a ghost could be trapped, so I decided on a piece of costume jewelry I owned that was made of pewter. It was not very spooky looking, and had been purchased from the back pages of a magazine with my allowance money.

Molly agreed to be put inside the piece of jewelry. I had read enough books about ghosts and worked with her enough that together we designed a ritual to transfer her spirit into the necklace for safekeeping and travel. I lit candles, danced and jumped around to raise energy, and placed the necklace on top of the Ouija board, chanting and calling for Molly to enter it. After the ritual, I picked up the necklace and felt a strange, freezing-cold sensation envelop my entire body, making my hairs stand on end. I was certain that Molly was inside the costume jewelry. I thanked her and promised that I would make sure that nothing bad happened to her, even though I was going to show her what school bullies were really like. I could barely sleep that night, excited to take Molly with me to school the next day.

In the morning, I doubted my plan. What if I was making all of this stuff up about the ghost in my necklace? Maybe I should just forget about it and never touch the necklace again. On the other hand, there was nothing to lose by wearing a random necklace I owned. I picked up the fetter and donned it, feeling an icy-cold chill touch my neck, as if the entire piece of jewelry had been placed in the freezer overnight.

That day in school, I did not tell anyone I was wearing a fetter. I was too afraid that even my good friends would make fun of me. Worse yet, the word could get out to my enemies. I did not take off the necklace, even during gym class in the locker room when I was showering and getting changed, trying not to meet eyes with the mean girls. One girl stopped and stared at the necklace I was wearing. "What is that?" She asked. "It's creepy." I stared at her. There was nothing creepy looking about the cheap pewter pendant, and it was probably one that I had worn a dozen times before without hearing any comment.

At lunch time, my boyfriend at the time saw the necklace and also made a comment. "Wow, that necklace is amazing. Can I have it?" I looked at him as if he had two heads. He didn't wear jewelry at all, and it didn't make sense that he would ask for my fetter. I mumbled something about how it was special to me and I didn't want to give it away. My boyfriend pressed further, asking if he could just borrow it for the next class period. His insistence was entirely unlike him, but I was smitten with my crush, so I agreed, making him promise to keep it safe.

He met me in the library after the next period to give me back my necklace, and looked entirely spooked. He said that he had heard strange voices when he was running on the track during gym class. Then, later in the locker room, some of the other boys had called him a witch and gotten in a fight with him, trying to steal the necklace. He was only too happy to give it back to me.

Finally, I went to my math class, where several bullies were waiting for me. This time, it was some older guys that always made lewd comments to me in class. They, however, seemed shocked to see me that day. A rumor had already reached them that my boyfriend had worn the necklace and displayed super-human abilities in a locker room fight. When they saw me wearing the fetter, they seemed frightened and gave me a wide berth. I managed to make it home that day without being bullied, so I never could show Molly an example of what it was like. I decided that it was probably a bad idea in the first place, and I never showed off the fetter at school again. Still, it was nice to think that I had a ghostly friend to help me stand up to bullies.

Contacting Mom

My friend Sarah came to my Halloween party with a specific person in mind she wanted to contact through the Ouija board. Sarah is deeply connected to her deceased mother, so much so that Sarah, a strong woman covered with tattoos, bears art on her body dedicated as a memorial to her mom. I paired up Sarah with my own mother, Jean, because I knew my mom would take the subject seriously and that she would consent to contact Sarah's deceased mom.

Several onlookers crowded around the table on which the Ouija board sat and respectfully watched the two women. As soon as their hands met on the Ouija board planchette, they jumped as if it were electrified. "I see her face," Jean said, her eyes squeezed shut with tears sliding down her cheeks. Sarah smiled. "I have head-to-toe goose bumps" she breathed. Everyone in the room felt a reaction. I heard one bystander whisper that she saw a smiling image, and even I felt a strange pull toward my own babies, who were sleeping upstairs.

Sarah asked, "Mama, are you with us now?" The planchette zipped to "yes" very quickly. "Mama, do you approve of this Ouija board?" The planchette shuddered, and Jean looked uncomfortable.

"What do you feel, Mom?" I whispered to my mother. "Anxiety," she answered. The planchette moved first to "yes" and then to "no" and then to the word "Ouija" printed on the logo of the board, prompting laughter from the room. Obviously she had conflicting feelings.

Sarah pressed on. "Mama, I have questions for you… Mama, do you see my husband?" The planchette moved to "goodbye" but Sarah, Jean, and others in the room still sensed her smiling. "Mama, do you see Shawn as I see Shawn?" The planchette darted back and forth between "no" and "yes." Curiously, both women at the board suddenly experienced an onset of pain. They winced and shifted, prompting a pause during which we found that they both had pain in the back and shoulders, where, as it happens, Sarah's mom had suffered chronic pain in life. They returned to the board.

"Mama, I have another question… Do you have a short answer for me, advice as to my beloved husband?" The planchette jittered and danced across the board. "I… we… PAIN." Again, the two women were bent over with the sensation of pain in the shoulders and back. They paused to discuss and determined that Sarah's mom's disapproval of the Ouija board was at fault. Their hands left the planchette and they joined hands over the board instead. It was then that they felt her answers coming as words into their minds, and they spoke words in rapid succession, each taking turns but seeming to form a disjointed whole and tumbling sentence.

"Instinct."

"Love."

"My heart swells."

The refrain of a song about love keeping two people together floated through the minds of everyone in the room, and Sarah said her mom was laughing. She turned to a more serious subject for her mom. "Will you visit my siblings, please?" Jean answered for her.

"They aren't open."

"Debbie is open," Sarah urged.

"Wrong time" was the answer.

"Are you happy there?" Sarah laughed as the answer was obvious that she was. "Mama, do you have your sisters?" There was a pause as she received her answer silently. "Well, that's one reason why you are happy!" The women wiped tears from their eyes. "Mama, I will be with you again very soon. Thank you for sharing the Ouija board that I know you don't approve of." As the ladies released their hands, Jean conveyed the parting words, "Not too soon." She could still hear the mom's laughter.

Ouija Board as Plain Fun

I would be remiss if I were to leave out stories of those people who don't believe in the Ouija board as spirit communication but still love to play with it as a simple game. The Ouija board can be a prop to start a practical joke on a superstitious friend, or a fun bonding experience and rite of passage in childhood. Of all the atheists and agnostics I spoke with who did not believe in ghosts, none of them thought the Ouija board should be banned from use by adults or children. One commented, "What harm could possibly come of it?" In the same breath, many regarded the Ouija board as silly and pointless. Of all the non-believers who were or were not fooled by the Ouija board early in life, none felt traumatized and all had fond, funny memories.

In the course of my research for this book, half the people surveyed were parents. Of course, no people were represented who disagreed with the use of the Ouija board, because all were planning to participate, so I got a rather odd community sample. None thought that children shouldn't have access to the Ouija board. Those who were skeptics thought it was just a fun childhood game that shouldn't be missed. Believers strongly felt that children should be allowed to explore spirituality freely. It must be said, however, that one of my friends did not participate because she wouldn't bring her seven-year-old daughter near a Ouija board, and she couldn't get a babysitter. Since her daughter gets scared by spooky movies, her mother thought the Ouija board might freak her out and give her bad dreams.

It seems like one valid reason for not allowing children access is if the child will become particularly annoying by evangelizing use of the board or developing a phobia of spirits. A couple I know, Dani and Dan, said they wouldn't even want to let a particularly superstitious adult friend use the Ouija board. They laughed while imagining how spooked a specific mutual friend would be. "He would be so annoying," Dani sighed. As skeptics, they would find the constant rehashing of a Ouija board experience to be insufferable.

I am a parent myself as well as a big practitioner of witch-craft and a student of the occult. I would certainly never forbid my children from using the Ouija board, but I think my opin-ion is greatly influenced by my lack of belief in demons and pure evil in this world. In my belief system, our everyday land-scape is full of spiritual "fauna" that can't be entirely avoided, but can be addressed. I can respect parents who are attempting to protect their children from something they believe is imme-diately dangerous. If a parent didn't want his or her child using a Ouija board at my house, I would respect that parent's wishes.

Fun Stories from People Enjoying the Ouija Board

When I threw my first Ouija board party for adults, I thought I'd have a hard time getting some of my more skeptical friends to attend. Quite the contrary. I had seven skeptics show up and only two believers. Even when I paired two skeptics together and nothing happened, they had fun. Two of my friends who didn't know each other, Mark and Eileen, sat in a stalemate for an entire minute. I was about to give up, but then Mark snorted and they both burst into red-faced, uncontrollable laughter. "You just bought yourselves four more minutes," I said.

Laughing at death

You know how nonsequiturs can turn into inside jokes between family and friends that can last for years? For example, my best friend, who is like a sister to me, used to play a game with me when we were kids. We would look up a word in the dictionary and try to guess what it meant. For some reason, if we didn't know the answer, the guess would be "an ice age?" The game would cause the both of us to giggle uproariously, and it is fondly remembered and referenced to this day between us. The Ouija board was involved in similar jokes.

One such gag started with another toy, the Magic 8-Ball. My best friend and I were asking it silly questions about how we were going to die. My friend didn't believe in divination at all, and though I did, I wasn't afraid of the answers, since I figure we have some leeway in choosing our life paths that could lead to an early (or delayed) demise. Besides, the Magic 8-Ball was very limited, having only positive or negative "yes" or "no" style responses, and we were asking about only very silly causes of death.

Finally, my best friend asked if I was going to die by drowning in Mop Mate, a cleaning product that happened to be nearby. The Magic 8-Ball responded simply "yes." We asked the question over and over again and, defying probability, the Magic 8-Ball answered always in the affirmative. We laughed and crowed about the joke all day long to our friends and parents.

Later that year, another friend decided that she wanted to investigate her own death with the Ouija board. When we asked how I would die, it spelled out "drowned." I had almost forgotten the joke with the Magic 8-Ball, so when I saw that I smiled and asked, "Will I drown in Mop Mate?" Sure enough, the planchette went to "yes" and I laughed. My friend, however, was horrified. She hadn't heard our terrible joke session previously, and was upset that I was confronting death with such a cavalier attitude. My best friend and I still remember the joke to this day, and I make sure to use nontoxic cleaning products just in case.

A trash-talking spirit

My skeptic friend Sarah came to a party at which a Ouija board was being played, ready to have fun. She was wearing a pin from her living grandmother, whom the family called G. B., but Sarah said, "I don't know too many dead people, and the dead people I know I don't know very well!" Sitting down to play with another skeptic at the Ouija board, she asked, "Is there a spirit present?" Sarah asked the question slowly, as per the manufacturer's instructions. The planchette didn't go to "yes" but instead spelled out "us." Sarah laughed, thinking, "Of course it is us two using the board. Maybe we have a message for us." She decided to ask aloud, "What is the message for us?" As they concentrated, the board spelled out what Sarah perceived to be a profane but funny message about her living grandmother, "F. U., G. B." the board said.

Sarah laughed and explained that her grandma G. B. was a bigot who did not approve of another family member's marriage; just about every other living family member strongly disapproved of G. B.'s stance on the matter. Perhaps a deceased family member shared the general family point of view. Or maybe the message was just Sarah's subconscious anger about a relevant part of her life. Either way, Sarah came away from the Ouija board laughing and telling everyone that it swore at her grandmother.

A cursing spirit

Halloween was always a very special time in Ani's family, and they loved anything to do with magic, from Harry Houdini to Ouija boards. In fact, Ani's mother bought the family Ouija board. At age sixty-two, Ani still fondly recalls many hours playing with the Ouija board with her brother, although the details became a bit fuzzy.

Back in her childhood, Ani was often courted by boys who were short, because she was small and nonthreatening herself. One such boy was named Jimmy. An Episcopalian, Jimmy was extremely skeptical of the Ouija board. However, he agreed to play with Ani and her brother.

Much to everyone's surprise, the Ouija board didn't seem to take kindly to a nonbeliever. It began to spell out profanity the likes of which a sweet young girl like Ani had never seen. Jimmy stepped back from the board fearfully but with blustering anger. "I'm not touching that thing!" he shouted, and left. Ani and her brother thought the whole exchange was hilarious. Though Ani was willing to play with the Ouija board again, her friend Jimmy was turned off of the Ouija board, and her, for good.

Portrait of a ten-year-old

At a Halloween party, a mom sat opposite her daughter, Gwen, at a Ouija board, and the questions Gwen asked sounded pretty typical of all of the childhood memories I've heard from adults.

"Does Bishop like Gwen?" The planchette pointed to the letter "G" and then to "yes." "Does Huntley like me?" Again it moved to "yes" while Gwen giggled and looked away. But it pointed to "no" when she asked if he loved her. She asked, "Does Quinsado like me?" Again, the pointer pointed to "yes." After that, though, Gwen's line of questioning left the planchette sitting on the board like a dead fish.

"Will I get a lot of candy for Halloween?" When she got no response, Gwen decided to ask it how to spell words that she didn't know how to spell. No movement. "Will Derek keep scaring me with his creepy clown costume?" Nothing. Gwen's mom laughed and said, "Looks like it is unwilling to predict things you will learn within the next three days."

Practical jokers

When I first told my husband I was writing a book on Ouija boards, he recalled with a smile a number of hazy memories of party fun as a teenager. With complete disregard for the paranormal or the spiritual, as a teen he had used the Ouija board to mess with his friends' minds. In a basement party filled with the smoke of stolen cigarettes and the smell of cheap beer, a group of friends would gang up on a more gullible member of the party. Deliberately moving the planchette to spell out words on the board, the game would start out with some plausible messages from a made-up spirit, and then progress to preposterous stories and hilarious insults. Once the jig was up and the originally gullible friend realized he or she had been played, everyone would laugh and abandon the activity for something else.

A sexy spirit

When Charity was about fourteen years old, she got together with three other friends and watched scary movies all night long. Then they used the Ouija board and decided to have some serious fun calling up spirits. Charity was excited, and they moved through many questions while trying to find out which spirits might be present. The other girls got a little annoyed when Charity consciously pushed the planchette to "goodbye" when she was done speaking with one spirit so she could move on to the next. She had other ghosts to talk to, after all.

At last, the giggling girls found a spirit they could all enjoy. She was a young and curious teenage spirit who had died before she could experience sex for the first time. The planchette moved in erotic spirals and strokes, much to the titillation of the girls using the board. A sense of sexually charged excitement filled the room. No real messages came through, however, and eventually the teenagers got bored and moved on to a more mundane party activity, leaving the foreplay with a spirit as a happy memory for all to take into young adulthood.

Silly questions irritate spirits

A woman named Tonya attended my second grown-up Ouija board party. She is a professed Christian who was raised Baptist, but she doesn't believe the Ouija board is anything more than a game. Carol, an onlooker at the Ouija board party, agreed. "I think the demons have better things to do," she said. Tonya's use of the Ouija board was pretty unique compared to most players. Instead of lightly touching the planchette and attempting not to consciously move it, she pushed it around the board speedily, not taking the time to plan its direction. The result was some pretty clear and hurriedly spelled messages from the Ouija board.

Tonya quickly determined that "Red, Tonya's friend long time" was the name of the spirit in the Ouija board and that it was the same spirit who had lived in the board when she was a teenager, and that wherever it wanted to go, it would go. Tonya paused the game to laugh a bit about her teenaged memories of the Ouija board. She used to play with her cousins, and after the game her cousins would make up fantastical stories about how the planchette had been on fire and had flown around the board. Of course, the planchette had never actually flown. The most that ever happened was that the planchette flipped right off the board.

Conversation in the Ouija board room turned to a discussion about whether children should be allowed access to the Ouija board, so Tonya decided to ask the board itself. "No, children would not be harmed," Red said. "Okay, kids should play. Nothing could happen to a kid using the Ouija board." Tonya laughed and added that there would be no fire and the planchette would not fly, as her cousins had claimed.

I asked Tonya what she thought happened after death, and she said she thought that we go to either heaven or hell. I asked if she thought she could call the devil to the Ouija board. The planchette raced to "no," confirming that we could not talk to the devil. The planchette's movements became jerky and it moved even faster. "Why are you so angry?" Tonya asked. "Bad day" the Ouija board replied. Two other spirits came through the board that session. One, called "D," who clarified that he was not the devil, and another, named "Q," came just in time for some more silly questions.

"Who is going to get elected?" We asked because the November 2012 presidential elections were forthcoming. Q answered that Obama would be reelected. "Will there be any natural disasters soon?" Q replied to the negative, but the planchette resumed its angry movements. When we asked why Q was so angry, he said that he didn't know why, but that there was no therapy for ghosts. We laughed. The final question that

Q would allow to be answered was, "Why do some people hate the Ouija board?" Q spelled out the word "ignorant" and then moved the planchette to "goodbye."

Women and men

One night at a party, the Ouija board was being enjoyed by many participants, but it was observed that attendees were mostly women. The only two men present that night, Herb and Derek, were encouraged to use the Ouija board together, so they agreed to do so, but not before Herb and his wife had a session together.

When Herb sat down at the board with his wife, he decided to have fun by asking some questions that would be uncomfortable for her. Their two kids were young adults, so he asked, "Will I be a grandfather within ten years?" The planchette replied, "Yes, 1 boy, yes." But, when asked if there was anything to know about their kids within the next year, it replied with nonsense: "8T." Confused, Herb switched out his Ouija board partner and tried again with Derek.

At first, none of the questions seemed to move the planchette. "Which of my children is going to be the first to give me a grandchild?" No response. Derek asked, "Will our old house sell in February?" Still nothing. Laughing, Herb called his wife back in the room, since she seemed to be the one who got the board hopping. Derek paired up with Herb's wife and he asked, "What should we do to help the sale of the house?" The Ouija board spelled out the word "yard," to which Derek snorted and said, "That's obvious." Then the board said, "Guv gut jewl…" which didn't make much sense. The two laughed at the idea of gutting the house, and Derek said the gutters were already doing fine.

The board indicated that the house would be sold to yuppies with no kids.

Herb's wife asked one of her own questions before trading places with Herb. She asked whether she would be given full-time hours at work, and the planchette indicated "yes." She was actually disappointed by the answer and moaned, "Oh no, I'm going to lose my days!"

Herb plopped back down in the seat that she vacated and asked again, "Is my daughter going to get pregnant within the next ten years?" The board spelled out "vex" to much laughter. Perhaps his constant prodding was annoying more than just his wife. The board spelled out nonsense: "5…3…M" so Herb changed topics. "At what age will I retire?" Again, the planchette wandered aimlessly. "Fx…7 Q…" Herb sighed and asked, "Will I die before I retire?" He was relieved that the answer was a clear "no," but he and Derek decided that they were bored with the slow-moving Ouija board.

Herb's wife, however, remembered her short and fun experience that day. Two days after the party her boss pulled her aside to tell her that he was just given approval to make her job full time. She would be a permanent, full-time employee within a month. The Ouija board had been correct.

Boy-crazy Ouija board players

My own vague memories of slumber parties and teenage girls using the Ouija board are mostly of the girls asking whether specific boys liked them. This seems like a pretty common line of questioning that forged a fond memory that has lasted a lifetime. Trish, now sixty years old, recalled for me some happy memories of playing with a Ouija board with her sister, Pam, who tragically died when Trish was only thirteen years old.

When Trish was only five years old, her family moved into an old farmhouse and discovered a Ouija board left behind by children who had lived there before. Trish and her sister sat cross-legged with the board balanced between them on their knees. Trish remembered the connection between her and her sister feeling like a circle, with their knees touching and their hands on the planchette.

Pam had been a boy-crazy preteen, so she asked countless questions that, at the time, went over Trish's head. Whether specific boys liked her or wanted to kiss her, or might secretly sneak away with her. Just when Trish was starting to get bored, Pam asked it, "Who are you, Ouija?" The reply was simply, "The boy who died here." Though Pam hadn't gotten her wish to find connection with the local boys she liked, the two sisters forged a memory together by contacting a boy who was a spirit, who identified himself as "Lee," said he liked to play ball, and missed his mother.

That night, a terrible thunderstorm frightened little Trish out of her bed. Her dad comforted her and suggested that she climb in bed with her big sister if she couldn't sleep. Pam lifted the covers and Trish dove into bed and fell fast asleep. Later that night, Pam shook her awake. "Do you see that boy in the chair?" she asked. Trish and Pam gazed over at the chair in Pam's room. A small boy sat in the chair, bathed in a golden hazy light. He wore a checkered shirt in a blue color that filtered through the golden glow. The boy was playfully engrossed with tossing and catching a golden ball. Over and over the ball went up and down, hypnotically, as the girls watched unafraid. Slowly, they each drifted back to sleep with their ghostly friend still in the room.

When they awoke, Lee was gone. At breakfast, the girls chattered excitedly about the boy, wondering if it was some trick that their father had played, which he denied. Their parents were confused and slightly concerned, but since neither girl seemed frightened, the conversation changed as the encounter was probably thought to be a child's flight of fancy. Though forgotten by their parents, the sisters often talked about the golden boy named Lee, all the way up until Pam's death. They had shared a magical moment, and the Ouija board seemed to have been the object to bring it about.

When Trish was thirteen, she made her own Ouija board out of ink on paper and the plastic cartridge from a Scotch tape dispenser. She used it on her own, asking, "Who are you, Ouija?" She consistently received messages from a spirit that spelled out its name "Demon" but it said that it was good, and had information about who was in heaven. Recalling this as an adult, Trish laughingly said, "Either I had a mischievous spirit called Demon working with me, or my tape dispenser had a serious sense of the macabre." Whatever it was, Trish was certain she was not the one moving her makeshift planchette, even during solitary sessions.

Excited about her Ouija board creation, young Trish asked her mother to play with her. When the devout Baptist saw the Ouija board spirit identifying itself as Demon, she began to pray loudly. Trish shook her head, saying "No, not a real demon, Mom." Then, thinking about her spiritual grandmother, she added, "Just one of God's creatures, so calm down." Trish's mom then asked about Pam, who had recently passed away, and Demon told them that Pam was in heaven, and they would see her soon. Trish wasn't worried about the "soon" since she had observed that the Ouija board seemed to experience time differently.

Trish's mom only cheered up when the Ouija board answered a few questions in an absurd manner. "Will I get married?" Trish asked. "Yes, many times" the Ouija board said. When Trish followed up, asking how many children she'd have, the Ouija board said there would be seventeen. Though at the time they had assumed the session was becoming more on the joking side, Trish shared with me as an adult that she has been married four times and has owned seventeen cats she always considered part of the family. Perhaps the Ouija board sprinkles a little truth into its humor at times.

True, Creeptastic Tales of the Ouija Board

For some, the Ouija board is not just fun and games. Spooky experiences don't happen only to those who have religious objections to the Ouija board. Sometimes terrifying encounters can happen amongst a few kids trying to have a good time with a game.

A lonely ghost

"It's all in your head," said my boyfriend, as we went to my house after high school had ended that day. I had my heart set on playing with the new Ouija board I bought at my job at the game store. The parents who came in to return boards they claimed were "cursed" and bad for their children had only intrigued me, and made me want one of my own. My boyfriend continued to tell me that it would just be my own hands moving the planchette to the letters I wanted to see. I sighed impatiently, wishing somebody with a little more sense of adventure would play with me.

"Fine," I countered, "What if I promise to keep my eyes closed and you just tell me what it says?" Seeing that I couldn't be dissuaded, my boyfriend reluctantly agreed. When we arrived home, I pulled out the Ouija board in all its paper glory, and was reminded to find a scarf that would act as a suitable blindfold for me. I lit some candles, but since my companion could stand no further pretentious ceremony, we began. Blindfolded, I sat across from him at a table as he peered over the board to identify what words were being spelled.

I remember the planchette moving a lot faster than I expected. Zipping underneath my fingers like a timid mouse, it seemed almost like it would scurry right off the board. My boyfriend growled at me to stop purposely pushing it so fast, and I tried to lighten my touch so that I was barely brushing the plastic with my fingertips.

The spirit identified herself as Molly Blakeland LaRue. She claimed that she had lived on our property and had died of consumption. "Does that mean she was eaten by something?" asked my boyfriend. He was obviously imagining somebody being devoured by wolves a hundred years ago.

"No," I said, "I think consumption is what they used to call tuberculosis." But he interrupted me, already enthralled, and made me continue. Next, the ghost indicated that she used to play in a band and attend Juanita High School back when it was a schoolhouse with children of mixed age. My boyfriend was hooked.

"What instrument did you play?" he asked excitedly. Then, narrating the letters that were being indicated, "F ... Oh, I think she's going to say French horn ... nope ... L-U-T-E. Flute! Wow, I wasn't even thinking that word. How did the board do that?" I had a few questions of my own, since I was curious about the afterlife. I asked her if she spent time playing with other people on the Ouija board, and she answered no.

I asked if she talked with other ghosts on the other side, and was dismayed when she said that we were the first people she had spoken to since she died. A chill ran up my spine, and I felt a deep sadness for the spirit we'd called into the Ouija board. "I am so very alone," she wrote on the board. Suddenly the planchette slipped out of our grip and landed in my lap. Being blindfolded, I jumped with surprise as it hit me, and removed the scarf from my eyes. My boyfriend met my gaze, and he shifted uncomfortably as we both shared the thought of an eternity of isolation.

The first Ouija board Spiritualist medium

Pearl Curran was a young housewife in St. Louis. She had dropped out of school at the age of fourteen to get married and have a family, but didn't have children at the time and no job to call her own. Bored, she turned to a Ouija board for entertainment, having learned about it from some friends who were involved with the Spiritualist movement. Unlike her friends, though, Pearl's interest in the Ouija board existed even when she was home alone, not just at parties or Spiritualist gatherings. Pearl wanted more than just a parlor trick—she wanted a friend for life who would help stimulate her intellectually and maybe give her the attention that was missing in her life.

One hot summer night, Pearl met her lifelong spirit friend through the Ouija board. Alone in the dark, the planchette suddenly began moving more purposefully, and the words were more lucid than ever before. Strangely, the language seemed to be in a dialect of late-medieval English from the thirteenth century, although Pearl didn't know it at the time. All she knew was that the Ouija board was speaking to her in a strange language. With startlingly quick movements, the spirit started to tell a story. Pearl struggled to keep up.

The ghost she was speaking to was a woman named Patience Worth, born more than two centuries ago. Originally from Dorsetshire, England, Patience explained that she had traveled to America to start a new life in the colonies. Sadly, her hopes and dreams were short-lived. Soon after reaching America and setting up her home to prepare to live out a happy life, she was killed by Native Americans who felt threatened by Patience and her ilk.

Patience was well-spoken through the Ouija board, and her words seemed to flow and to be easy to understand despite the speed with which she indicated the letters. Pearl asked if she wanted to dictate some writing, so that Patience's words could be shared with others. Patience was happy to finally have a voice again, and Pearl was eager to find recognition and respect for intellectual works. Together, they formed a writing team, and Pearl focused all of her energies over the next five years into transcribing Patience's work. Public interest soared, and Pearl finally felt like she was doing something with her life.

Pearl's dream had come true, and she and Patience continued to be best friends as Pearl aged. Pearl finally became a mother at age thirty-nine, and that is when the friendship first started to falter. Pearl simply no longer had time for her solitary conversations with Patience. Though she did her best to continue to produce Patience's writing, the quality of their collaborated works diminished, and so public interest declined as well. When Pearl's husband died, it all but destroyed her relationship with Patience. Desperate to communicate with her husband in the same way as she did with Patience, but somehow seemingly unable to do so, Pearl was devastated. She eventually fell ill with pneumonia and died, taking all further communications with Patience with her.

Childhood fears remain

Kim remembered the Ouija board from his childhood trips to his grandparents' two-story farmhouse. The farmhouse was scary itself, with an open septic tank in the basement covered with plywood. Back in that day, Kim said that grandparents could make scary threats to children about throwing them in a cistern without being considered bad authority figures.

He and his cousins would play with the Ouija board in a game room at the top of a creaky staircase and at the far end of a dark hallway. A young aunt of his named Diane, only ten years older than most of the kids, would goad the kids into playing and help whip them up into a fearful frenzy.

"Our take on how the Ouija board worked," said Kim, "was that all would put hands on it, the pointer would miraculously slide, and then fights would break out!" He was, of course, referring to memories of everyone denying their own part in moving the planchette. Kim, to his credit, always played fair, which made him the target of the pranks of his cousins and Aunt Diane.

He was fooled many times. The worst part, he remembers, is that nobody would be brave enough to walk away from the Ouija board and end the game. After all, in order to do so, the brave kid would have to walk down the dark hallway and the creaky stairs alone, or convince another kid to come along.

Kim and his wife April both refused to come to my Ouija board parties because they both had fearful memories of the Ouija board. When April was in college, she spent all of her time hanging out with her theater friends. "Theater folks are freaky," she said.

Her own theater crew believed that the stage was haunted. Rumors traveled through the community of a young and abused boy who had run away from home and hidden himself away in a theater, dying there. After the old theater was demolished, the ghost of the boy moved into the new theater by the waterfront. Footsteps could be heard on the empty stage whenever anyone descended into the costume storage arae directly below. Stories of mishaps and things gone missing abounded and were blamed on the ghost.

One night, April and her theater friends made their own Ouija board, and managed to contact the ghost of the theater. The ghost was able to give corroborating information about its own history and the theater that the new people partici- pating didn't know, so it seemed like the phenomenon of the Ouija board was legitimate. Though time blurred the details, some of the details were proven beyond a doubt shortly after the Ouija board session, much to everyone's surprise.

April remembered that the ghost communicated through the Ouija board that he was unhappy with some of April's male friends in the theater picking on her. She thought it was rather nice to know that she had somebody looking out for her, but it was still a little freaky. Many of the theater folks were freaked out by the Ouija board experience, so much so that the handmade Ouija board may have been destroyed after its first use.

Not only do Kim and April refuse to use a Ouija board to this very day, but Kim reported a strange happening going on in my house after a Ouija board party had occurred. He came to take care of my dogs while my family was on vacation. The dogs were outdoors, so no living soul was in the house. Yet, every day that he arrived to feed and play with the dogs, a door would be open. Kim closed the door each time, and yet it would open again. When the topic of the Ouija board came up among friends, he remembered the mysterious opening door and it cemented his concerns about the Ouija board.

A haunted house

Patricia was experienced with Ouija boards, and always used them in her time of need. She had used homemade Ouija boards as well as the commercial variety, but vastly preferred those she constructed with her own hands. She said the difference was "like kissing your junior high boyfriend instead of your twenty-five-plus lover. They both are sincere but the spark just isn't there." Patricia hadn't had need to use a Ouija board until she and her husband fell upon hard times after buying a house for a startlingly low price.

Patricia bought a house that had been built in the early 1930s along with a couple of other homes on the property. Immediately after moving in, when they began renovations, they scraped off some paint to discover that the house had obviously experienced a pretty bad fire. Patricia discovered that the bedroom had been set on fire by the daughter of the original occupants in order to kill herself and her parents. They also learned a town rumor that animal abuse and sacrifices had occurred in the house's basement.

Patricia and her husband began noticing that the house had a few scary quirks. Aside from the usual moaning and groaning a settling house makes, light bulbs would explode at random. Ceiling tiles would droop and then fall. A black substance even oozed out of the kitchen ceiling. To top it all off, the entire house became infested with fleas. But the house was old, so Patricia thought all of the happenings were normal. She and her husband even discovered that a fault line ran directly under the unlucky house. Her neighbor in one of the other houses wasn't as patient with the mysterious problems; refrigerator motors regularly burned out, so she simply couldn't keep a refrigerator running at all. She moved out after a night when all of the light bulbs in her house exploded.

Patricia and her husband stayed for years, but their luck kept getting worse and worse. Everyone in the house was depressed; even their pets were sad. Patricia and her husband were unable to sleep. As insomnia gripped them tightly, they couldn't find rest and peace for any more than an hour for over a year. Finances worsened considerably, and finally they were no longer able to make their house payment. The depression culminated when Patricia became so despondent that she was driven to attempt suicide. In a moment of desperation, she and her husband decided to turn to the Ouija board for answers because she badly wanted help with her finances. To this day, she believes that her desire for personal gain was the wrong reason to consult the Ouija board.

When a spirit came to the board immediately, it said, "I am the demon of this time and place." They asked for its help, and the demon agreed. They asked for winning lottery numbers, and the Ouija board began giving numbers at once, but there were far too many. Patricia and her husband wrote them all down anyway, hoping to use them in different combinations to win. The demon must have had no love for them, because they didn't win a cent.

It was then that Patricia decided to go to a palm reader. Before she even sat down to explain her situation, the reader started with this startling advice, "You are surrounded by the blackest of clouds. Wherever you are living, you need to move out now." The reader grasped Patricia's palm and knew about Patricia's work with the Ouija board, telling her that Patricia was sensitive to things that the Ouija board could bring forth from beyond, but that she couldn't control them. Before using the Ouija board again, the reader advised Patricia that she had to either learn to become stronger, or to build a "fort" to keep it all out.

One week later, Patricia and her husband moved out of the haunted house. The day of the move was dramatic, with wind howling down the chimney, mysterious creaks and bumps following them around the house, and light bulbs bursting when they first entered each room. Patricia left the house and her use of the Ouija board in the past. Though she hasn't used a Ouija board in decades, when asked if she would use one again, her answer was a curiously clear affirmative: "I wouldn't hesitate!"

Possession

Rayne was nine years old when she played with the Ouija board with her two friends, Amanda and Jennifer. The three girls sat in a triangle configuration with the Ouija board resting in the middle and used it as a group. They prodded the Ouija board with questions that only they knew the answers to, in order to see whether it would always tell the truth. Startlingly, it did, and they were soon scared and convinced that there was a spirit in the board.

The three girls joined hands to ask the next question, mimicking a séance that they had heard about in movies. "Great spirits, great spirits, what is your name?" They chanted the question and waited a moment, hands still joined. Suddenly, all three girls blurted out the same name aloud in unison, "Julie!" This spooked all three of them greatly, and Rayne had a sneaky idea. She decided that she would pretend to be possessed by Julie.

The other two girls were convinced, and Rayne was soon chasing Amanda and Jennifer out of the house and down a gravel road on a hill while her brother watched quizzically and laughed. Rayne was frenzied and her friends felt real fear as they half ran, half tumbled away from her. Rayne's feet flew as she pounded down the hill, but then suddenly, at the bottom of the hill, she came to an unnaturally quick stop as if she had slammed into an invisible wall. She didn't even skid or trip on the gravel as her feet rooted to the ground. She screamed that she couldn't move, but Amanda and Jennifer wouldn't come closer. Obviously they were afraid that their friend was still possessed by something dangerous, and curious as to whether the spirit of Julie was playing some kind of trick to catch them.

Rayne looked down at her feet and noticed that somebody seemed to have built an inlaid cross in the middle of this road at the bottom of this hill. A cross in different colored stones seemed to jump out of the drab gray gravel. She hadn't noticed the cross while she was running, and now she seemed physically unable to move past it. Rayne was able to back away from the cross and return home. She begged her brother to tell her that he had played a trick on her somehow, but he had no idea what was going on or who had laid that cross in the road. The moral of the story, Rayne says, is "Don't ever pretend you're possessed, because it just might be true."

As an adult, Rayne attended a Halloween party of mine with her husband Jason, and they used the Ouija board together. When the board revealed that a male spirit was present, gave its age as seventy-three and said that it was standing next to somebody in the room, Rayne began to feel sick to her stomach, as if she was going to throw up. Jason asked, "Are you at peace?" She started shaking and the hairs on the back of her arms were standing on end. She felt frightened, and was happy to end the session when the spirit bid her goodbye by spelling, "Tata."

In the air tonight

An author named Dustin shared this true story with me, which he wrote about after remembering a real Ouija board experience from his days back in college. As you get absorbed in this story, you'll see how startling experiences with the Ouija board can make memories of small paranormal moments come together in an instant to form an understanding of death and destiny. It is amazing how a few moments with a Ouija board can make the memories of surrounding events more sharp and meaningful.

Dustin's sister Kate's apartment in Boston's Beacon Hill was on the top floor of a six-story walk-up, and all of 150 square feet! It was early September 1976 when Kate, Lena, and Dustin sat in Kate's living room. It was a magical time to be on the Hill, where the past still echoed down its narrow cobblestone streets. Colonial stables and storefronts hadn't yet transformed into the pricey condos and lofts they would be in the 1980s. The Bull and Finch remained a quaint neighborhood bar, and not the tourist mecca it would later become selling *Cheers* souvenirs.

Every inch of Kate's tiny flat was crammed with antiques, a stereo, hot plate, TV, dining room table, LPs, oil paintings, and a wicker basket filled with her dog Ginger's well-chewed bones. A cast-iron Franklin stove stood away from the wall, which Kate kept stoked and burning during the winter.

She also kept an old Ouija board tucked away on a bookshelf alongside her albums. Earlier that day she told Dustin how, when she last used the mysterious game, the planchette had moved on its own; her hands were supposedly inches above the tan plastic pointer as it mysteriously spelled out the name of a boy named Cameron.

Kate was known as a dramatic person, so Dustin took her story with a grain of salt. But that night he felt compelled to needle her about it as part of his sworn oath to be an obnoxious baby brother. "Well, if this is really true, do you think you could do it again? Maybe we can ... "

"Oh no," she said, interrupting him. "No. It really freaked me out. I haven't touched the board since. I don't want to talk about it." Dustin smiled and looked at her with a mixture of *I-understand, I-don't-care, I-don't-believe-you,* and *I-want-to-use-that-thing-no-matter-what.* Lena sat in the corner confused as the two siblings discussed something incomprehensible.

Kate looked down and dug her toes nervously into the graying white carpet as her brother cajoled her some more. "I said I don't want to," she repeated, becoming peeved. Dustin saw an opening for manipulation.

"I understand," he said. "It must have been frightening." The room went quiet. After a moment, Dustin mumbled, "…if it really happened."

Kate sighed loudly, hauled herself up to her feet, and took the old cardboard box from the shelf to lay it on the floor. Dustin squirmed nervously with anticipation. As much as he secretly didn't believe her, another part of him knew she was telling the truth. Some weird things had happened to Dustin, too. Two years before, in Denver, he spontaneously began automatic writing and described how his best friend Billy would die in a car crash the next day, two thousand miles away in Pittsburgh.

Billy lies on the street
Head beside an overturned Jeep
No we will never meet
Again—till the end

Dustin had no conscious idea whatsoever of what he'd written until he came back to Denver after Billy's funeral and saw the scribbled notes still beside the telephone where he'd feverishly tried to call Billy all that day for no apparent reason.

Understandably, Billy's untimely death became fresh in Dustin's mind as the three of them gently laid their hands on the felt-tipped pointer and attempted communion with the spiritual realm.

"Is there someone here who wants to speak," Kate inquired. The planchette effortlessly slid to "Yes." Lena squealed but Dustin rolled his eyes, assuming Kate moved it on her own. It was just too obvious. Plus, he didn't get any chills or whatever-you're-supposed-to-feel from the other side. After a few minutes the board went quiet when Dustin got an idea: "Let's see if my friend Billy is here."

The words "hey Billy, you here?" were barely out of Dustin's mouth when the planchette abruptly moved to "yes." Dustin was startled but suspicious, and also had to assume Kate would never fake anything like that, something still so painful for her brother. Dustin wondered what to ask next when he remembered that the recently departed often attend their own funerals. He ask Billy if he had been present at his funeral. "Yes," said the pointer. "Did you see me there?" Dustin queried naively, still speechless from this unexpected development. The pointer slowly circled the board and then landed squarely on "yes."

Ever distrustful, Dustin needed proof positive, some telltale sign only he would know. Dustin got a strange idea: he said to Billy in my head, *Well, if it really is you then make me cry.* No sooner did he place his hands on the pointer when tears started gushing from his eyes. Within seconds, Dustin looked like someone threw a glass of water on him.

The two girls reached out to comfort him, rubbing his back consolingly and telling him it was okay. "No! No, I'm not upset!" he said. "Look, I'm laughing, see?" They smiled at him

with a knowing look, assuming that he was obviously just trying to put up a good front. Then he shared with them what he
silently asked Billy to do, pointing at the tears on his cheeks.

"I'm crying but I'm not crying. See? It's crazy, I can't stop it!
Okay, okay, Billy!" Dustin yelled through the torrents of tears.
"That's enough. Stop it!"

Abruptly, the tears discontinued as quickly as they started.
And Dustin could swear he saw Billy laughing in his mind's
eye. Catching his breath, Dustin took in great gulps of air
and gradually realized that maybe Billy really was there in the
room. Feeling numb, Dustin couldn't think of anything more
to ask. The three gently placed their hands back on the planchette as it slowly started to move. Just as the pointer landed on
"goodbye," the twelve-pound grate covering the Franklin stove
flew off its hinges and went airborne, soaring seven feet across
the room and crashing with a thunderous clang.

Lena screamed, Ginger bolted, and Kate instinctively ducked
her head to keep from getting hit. Dustin was frozen and silent.
As the shrieks and yelps settled down, he quietly whispered, "Bye,
Billy. Thank you."

Lena moved back into her chair and said that she never
would have believed this if she hadn't seen it with her own
eyes. Dustin told them more about his friend and the automatic writing experience two years prior. At the time, he was
confused as to why he had flown directly to Colorado after
his first year in college and not gone home to Pittsburgh. It
was unthinkable that Dustin wouldn't first go and see his best
friend. They had been inseparable. But if Dustin had returned
to Pittsburgh, he surely would have been with Billy that night

in the Jeep, without a doubt. Instead Dustin had inexplicably flown to Denver.

Remembering, Dustin shook his head and muttered how Billy's strange high school senior quote now seemed almost prescient. As Dustin's unfinished thought was still hanging in the air, in a cautious whisper Lena asked, "What was his senior quote?" A lump formed in Dustin's throat. "Planes still fly from Denver," he said, holding back real tears.

The occult spilling into regular life

Nicole was interested in everything magical. When she was seventeen, she felt she had outgrown "Disney-fied" magic, and wanted to learn more about everything that was magical and mysterious in the real world. Were there real magic words that could be said to change the world? Through the library, a whole new realm of books about Satanism and witchcraft beckoned to her. She decorated her room with leering gargoyles, colored candles, and a Ouija board, using it to try to learn real magic words.

One night, after using the Ouija board, she fell into a fitful sleep. When she awoke with a shout, she sat bolt upright in bed and looked at a candle sitting on her nightstand. A smoldering ember on the wick ignited and the flame arose brightly. Nicole quickly extinguished it, thinking about how odd it was that the candle seemed to light itself. It must not have been blown out entirely, she decided. She pinched the wick to make sure that no embers remained, and then went back to sleep. She continued her experiments with the Ouija board the next day without concern.

The next unusual incident came when Nicole had gotten into another of her frequent arguments with her parents. She stomped off to her room and slammed the door, releasing a frustrated yell. At that moment, a few stray papers on a table in her room suddenly caught fire. Nicole frantically stomped out the burning papers with a booted foot and wiped the ash from the table to inspect its minor black burn marks. Rattled, she got up and slammed the door to the room again, wondering if she could recreate whatever effects of the air blowing around the room had caused the phenomenon to occur. Nothing happened. Was there something magical going on, or had some entity come out of the Ouija board that was now playing tricks?

Nicole knew that her parents didn't mind her playing with the Ouija board, so she decided to go to them for advice. She approached her mother when she was cooking and asked her whether she'd ever had similar experiences, knowing that her mom had used Ouija boards in the past as well. Her mom nodded, still stirring dinner. "I had to learn how to stop things like that from happening in my own way," she said. "You'll need to figure out your own way as well." Nicole felt more lost than ever.

Even when she moved away to college, taking her occult supplies with her, strange incidents followed Nicole, or perhaps sought her out, as her dorm window overlooked a cemetery. In her dorm room, a glass by her bedside shattered itself, sending shards landing in a perfect circle around Nicole. Her roommate accused her of being evil, and hurriedly moved out before the year was up. The only thing that seemed to stop the tormenting phenomena was when Nicole found religion. By then, she had moved around enough that her Ouija board had been left behind, sold at a garage sale to some other unsuspecting soul.

Trying to save lives

Amy felt a lump in her throat as she watched live news coverage of the search and rescue operation for the plane piloted by John F. Kennedy, Jr. Parents and neighbors spoke somberly but excitedly about something so terrible happening to somebody famous, as if they were gossiping about a mutual acquaintance. Amy, however, felt sick to her stomach. There were real people in that plane, not just characters from a television show. She wondered if there was any way they could be saved or even if their bodies could be recovered. How could people be found in a vast ocean littered with wreckage? Was there any way for them to communicate their location in time? Amy thought she might just have the answer: her friend's Ouija board.

Heading over to her friend Colleen's house, Amy quickly explained her idea. Excited at the prospect of speaking with a celebrity, her friend immediately agreed. They got to work using the Ouija board together, begging the universe to somehow put them in contact with somebody who was on that plane. Immediately, they began to receive answers. Skipping the formalities of asking who was speaking through the board, Amy asked if there was anybody who was on that plane who was still alive, and the spirit talking through the board answered in the affirmative. She and Colleen exchanged excited glances, and Amy's heart jumped in her chest. Time was of the essence. Colleen asked the most important question of all, trying to find out the location of the wreckage so that anyone living could be saved. The planchette moved quickly and purposefully, but didn't seem to be spelling out actual words.

Their brows knit together in confusion. Frustrated, the girls repeated their question again and again. The planchette dutifully continued to spell out complete gibberish. Desperately, they tried to find their answers, but it was as if the consciousness that was coming through the board was being absorbed in the void of death or whatever was claiming those who had experienced the wreck. The girls were forced to abandon their attempt to save any survivors, and later they found out that, sadly, only bodies were found.

A spirit offering

Cielito considered herself to be a skeptic when she came to my Ouija board party, but she had experienced some mysterious things in life to which she didn't ascribe any particular meaning. For example, she once lived with a Haitian woman who believed in spirits. Her landlady told her that people who needed healing tended to come to live in her home, and indeed Cielito had been going through some tough emotional times and was in need of a period of rest and recovery. She left the home when she felt better, and when the woman claimed that spirits told her that it was time for her to move on. She respected her landlady's beliefs, and admired how she often gave the spirits food offerings. When Cielito came to my Ouija board party, she brought fresh fruit to share with the guests, an offering intended for the gathering's living spirits.

I was occupied with the business of orchestrating some serious Ouija board experiments. I had everyone identify themselves as either a skeptic or a believer, and started pairing everyone off in different combinations to see what would happen. I assumed that the skeptics wouldn't get anything, that the believers would get plenty of messages, and that the sessions that paired skeptics with believers would be hit-or-miss. I had no idea that Cielito's offering of fruit would play an important part in the proceedings that night.

We were off to a busy start when I paired a skeptic with a believer for the first session. The second session had two believers, and of course the messages were flying. Since we were on a roll, I paired two skeptics and we were all surprised when the planchette continued to spell messages. Another session went by with a skeptic and a believer and I was thrilled that we had not yet had a sitting where the planchette just sat there.

Finally, we did get the lull that I was expecting. There were two pairs of skeptics that waited out five minutes during which the planchette sat entirely stationary. Cielito, who had been munching on some sliced apples and cheese laughingly suggested, "Maybe the spirits are hungry!" Her turn was next and, being a skeptic, she was stepping up to the plate with a believer. She set a peach in the offering bowl, and they sat down to work. Both had seen the planchette move earlier in the evening, so even though Cielito still identified as a firm skeptic, I was hoping there were a few cracks in her cynical armor. She certainly seemed sincere when she asked, "Dear Ouija, what is the purpose of this evening?" But nothing happened and they waited out five minutes of a fixed planchette. Cielito laughed and joked that maybe the spirit was eating the peach.

Shockingly, activity on the Ouija board picked up immediately after Cielito gave up on that particular session. For the rest of the night, any people who sat at the Ouija board not only saw planchette movement, but even more clear messages produced more quickly than ever before. I was surprised, because

I assumed that it would be the beliefs of the people sitting at the board that dictated its activity. But it was actually more correlated to the peach, since the only lull in activity happened with three sessions clumped together right before Cielito's offering.

Skeptic no more

Shannon came to the Ouija board party as a skeptic. She had only had one previous experience with the Ouija board, at summer camp as a kid. She remembered that experience to be painfully contrived, with it being obvious that the other girls were pushing and pulling the planchette to spell out silly messages. The only question she remembered was one a kid asked about what they were having for dinner, and the board spelled out "spaghetti"—completely unsurprising since everyone knew what was planned for dinner. As an adult, Shannon was more comfortable with facts and numbers, working as a bookkeeper and going to school to become an accountant. Still, she was a good sport about the Ouija board because she wanted to be nice to her friends and play along.

Shannon was first paired up with another skeptic, and they sat down together at the Ouija board. "Is there a spirit present?" Shannon asked the question slowly, as the instructions dictated on the game box. She felt a strange heaviness pressing down on her hand that made her feel uncomfortable. It seemed as if the planchette was being pulled away from her as it slid ironically to "no." Both skeptics blinked with surprise. Wanting to continue the game, Shannon asked, "What kind of entity are you?" The heaviness returned to her hand with renewed strength as the planchette slid unchecked around the letters, spelling "mfsst," apparently gibberish. Shannon felt extremely overwhelmed by the odd feeling in her hands and she let go, moving away from the board. She was done, but she felt like there was definitely something weird happening with the board. She left the room declaring that she wasn't a skeptic anymore.

A drowned boy

At my Ouija board party, my skeptical husband was paired up with a die-hard atheist skeptic. Happening to know some history about the next-door neighbor's defunct swimming pool, my husband asked, "Is the spirit of the young boy who drowned in the pool next door present?" Though the two of them waited, the planchette just wiggled spastically without any real message.

When the two skeptics emerged and mentioned the drowned boy, one of the believers at my party, Devlyn, got excited about it. She grabbed a skeptic for a partner and they sat down at the board. Before they even asked a question, the planchette moved to "yes" and Devlyn laughed and said she was just thinking, "Are we ready?" Both players closed their eyes entirely for the rest of the session. "What is the name of the boy who drowned?" Devlyn heard her partner complaining that her arms ached, but she kept her eyes squeezed shut as I recorded the results. The board spelled out "Paul."

The box claimed that the Ouija board could answer any question, so Devlyn wondered if it held wisdom about health matters. She asked, "Why do I keep getting a sore throat?" Her skeptical partner at the board laughed and asked, "Is the cause physical or psychological?" The planchette raced to "yes" and they both broke into peals of laughter. The board wasn't finished yet. "Need to profvs ssalef," it wrote. "It looks like the board is saying you need to prove yourself," I said, and the planchette raced to "yes" to confirm. Devlyn nodded with her eyes still closed. "I am having a hard time expressing…" she replied, and the planchette responded with another "yes."

The mood in the room had gotten rather sober, and the skeptic unexpectedly asked, "Does this apply to both of us?" The board answered "yes" again. The skeptic looked incredibly uncomfortable, and I sensed that we should bring the session to a close soon. Suddenly, the board wrote, "I love talk 2 you yes." By this time, the skeptic had gotten so freaked out that she pulled her hands away and left the session. Leaving the room, she asked my husband how old the boy who drowned had been. My husband said somewhere around age five.

Devlyn, however, was still excited to keep playing with the board. She grabbed a different skeptic and they headed back to the Ouija board so that Devlyn could ask some spiritual questions about the universe. Devlyn was a practicing Wiccan, and she wanted to know about things that could not be seen. "Tell us about realms," she said as both players closed their eyes and let me note down the answers. The Ouija board replied, "3, 3 more view yes."

"Does that mean there are four realms?" Devlyn asked to clarify. The Ouija board started to answer, spelling out "yes, f…", but Devlyn was already interrupting with more questions. "I want to know how many of them we can access." The board simply answered "yes."

Both women at the board kept their eyes closed and continued. "Is one of them the spirit realm?" The board agreed, but seemed to not make sense afterward, saying "yes, ufafcal…no…call fae." Devlyn noticed her hand feeling very heavy as she wondered aloud, "So, like, a fairy realm?"

The Ouija board was emphatic, although still confusing, saying "Yes, yes…ubw…yes!" The planchette was zipping around the board and confusing everyone in the room.

"Is there a question here?" Devlyn wondered. Again, the Ouija board indicated the affirmative and Devlyn laughed, asking "Is somebody having a really good time?" The Ouija board cheerfully responded, "yes, 6vo…"

Devlyn was still curious as to who was behind the messages they were receiving. "Is this Paul?" The Ouija board denied being the drowned boy. "Is this the spirit realm?" The heaviness on Devlyn's hand increased. "Is this the goddess?" The planchette zipped to "goodbye" and the session was over.

Do not disturb the Druids

Always fascinated with Pagan history, Cathy took a trip with her brother and parents to the United Kingdom when she was ten years old. Back then, visitors could walk right up to Stonehenge and interact with the ancient structure. She still remembers watching the sunrise and thinking about Stonehenge's history. Her father took a family photo in front of the stones and later had it enlarged to hang in a frame above the fireplace back home.

It was years later when Cathy, her brother, and a friend named Jacquie, whom Cathy had met on a subsequent trip to the United Kingdom, played with the Ouija board together in Cathy's family home. The Ouija board session seemed to be full of normal, mundane questions until the players turned to their common interest in Pagan history. "Are there any Druids about?"

The Ouija board emphatically informed them that they should not ask questions about such things. Playfully, they gently prodded with more questions about Druids while the Ouija board strongly resisted answering any of the questions and urged them to stop with such an intensity that it was unsettling. The three decided to stop playing, and it was then that Cathy noticed what had happened to the family photo in front of Stonehenge. The frame and photo remained undisturbed, hanging on the wall just as before the session, but a crack had formed straight down the center of the glass.

Sex

Rebecca and her best friend were high school kids when they played with the Ouija board. Naturally, the questions they asked were provocative and taboo in nature. When a spirit arrived in the board for them, they immediately began teasing and taunting it. "Do you miss sex?" The girls snickered.

As the hyperactive activities for the night died down, they both went to another room to lie down and go to sleep. In the quiet darkness of the room, they both heard a booming voice. Each thought it sounded like it was right next to her ear. It loudly said "SEX."

It was only one word, but it was said in a clear, deep, and vaguely threatening voice. Immediately the lights were switched on. The source of the voice could not be found. The girls drifted off into an unsettled sleep, only mildly comforted by a brightly lit room.

Hearing voices

This next story also includes the phenomenon of hearing voices. In order to protect her identity and that of her family, we'll call the subject of this story Katrina. Katrina was a teenager when she began using the Ouija board with friends. Her experiences while using the board were fairly typical. Spirits were called up and asked to answer various questions about the teenagers' lives and crushes. However, while using the board, Katrina heard a sinister voice whisper her name into her right ear. She became spooked and decided to stop using the board.

That night, when she returned home from a friend's house, she heard the voice again. This time it was louder and more insistent. Though she was afraid of what her conservative Baptist Christian parents would say, Katrina was too frightened not to ask for help. When she told her father, he immediately decided to perform an exorcism upon her.

Katrina was terrified. Her father shouted Bible verses at her in order to remove the demon from her body in the name of Jesus Christ, but she knew all this would be worth it if it worked. When the exorcism was over, Katrina was shaken, but she felt better. She never heard the voice again. The exorcism seemed to completely cure her spiritual affliction.

Dealing with the devil

When Loona first used a Ouija board with friends, she was dubious but excited. The only thing she knew about Ouija boards was that her mother had told her a story about how she once had used a Ouija board and the place where it had been used had remained haunted ever since. As Loona's first session with the Ouija board commenced, she soon became a believer.

Loona was able to talk with her deceased grandmother and felt a warmth as she used the board, as if her grandmother was smiling lovingly at her once again. Loona's grandmother gave her advice through the board, helping with family disputes between Loona and her parents as well as between Loona's cousin and her stepfather, even though the two of them were not present. However, that night the Ouija board wasn't just heartwarming.

During Loona's session, the board said that it was channeling the devil. Suddenly, she felt the temperature in the room rise rapidly to an uncomfortable level, as if it were surrounded by the fires of hell itself. Loona wanted to stop using the Ouija board, but felt as though she couldn't. She was being sucked into the game as if it were an attractive lover. In fact, against her will, she began experiencing sexual feelings. Her mind raced to myths and legends about witches cavorting with the devil, and receiving his mark as a mole or spot from their impassioned embraces.

Finally, Loona realized that she'd had enough. Overcoming the strange force that was keeping her trapped in the game, she forcibly pushed the planchette to "goodbye." Her friends were angry that Loona had consciously moved the planchette. Obviously they too had been drawn in by the charm of the devil in the board.

Loona's time with the devil wasn't over, however. Every time she used the Ouija board, she had trouble falling asleep. She heard mysterious footsteps pacing the hallways and felt chills creeping up her spine, as if somebody were watching her from the dark corners of her bedroom. Her dreams were haunted by the devil, too. In lucid dreams that felt more like a hypnotic trance state than sleep, she felt as if she were stolen away to the world of demons to be the devil's bride. Each night, kidnapped in fear, she was unable to escape this infinite loop of nocturnal torture until finally a ritual was performed in her home to banish the evil presence the Ouija board had invoked.

Demon-possessed house

Lee had a story from her past about the Ouija board that still haunts her family to this very day, even though it occurred when she was only thirteen years old, on her thirteenth birthday, in fact. Lee decided to have a party in which many party games would be played that toyed with the occult. Five boys and seven girls were present, giggling and flirting and having a fun time scaring each other.

They started out with what Lee recalled as "the candle game," in which they would attempt to summon different spirits and entities. If the candle flared up, the creature summoned would be supposed to be present. Questions could be then asked about people sitting around the candle, and the candle would answer by pointing its flame toward one person or another. During the candle game, each of the teens was sufficiently frightened. Finally, one of the bolder kids shouted, "I summon the devil!" The candle flame leapt so high that it seemed to lick the noses of the frightened kids. Terrified, everyone ran screaming from the room, and Lee thought that it was time for another party game. She got out the Ouija board.

Playing with the Ouija board actually calmed everybody down, because each person could ask a question to which everyone really knew the answer. Of course, at that age, everyone was asking questions about who had a crush on whom, and that sort of information is common knowledge. Lee quickly grew bored bored the ordinary nature of the answers, so she wanted to ask a question that nobody else would know. Since Lee happened to have a middle name she never shares that has a very unusual spelling, she asked the Ouija board to prove that it worked by spelling it for everyone. The Ouija board spelled it exactly, which spooked Lee to the core. This time it was she who wanted to end the game and move on to another.

After the Ouija board had opened their minds even wider, the children decided to play a game called "light as a feather, stiff as a board." In this game, one person would lie down on the floor as if dead. The others would surround the prone participant, each placing one or two fingers underneath or at his or her side. Chanting "light as a feather, stiff as a board" was supposed to make the prone person levitate upon the fingers of the other participants. For the game that night, Lee's little brother was tapped to play the dead person. As the chanting of "light as a feather, stiff as a board" whipped into a frenzy, the teens were surprised and delighted when their fingers easily lifted Lee's little brother as if he weighed nothing.

When the chanting died down, their fingers were slowly drawn away and Lee's little brother continued to hang suspended from midair, like a floating corpse. In fact, nobody could seem to get him down from there, even by pulling downward on his body forcefully. Finally, the poor boy screamed, which seemed to release him, and he fell safely to the floor.

Ever since that night, Lee said, "My house was infested with energetic bad things." They took over the house. Stomping feet were heard in the attic and especially in Lee's bedroom, where the Ouija board had been used. Objects would fly through the air. Doors would open and close on their own. Lee remembered several terrifying incidents that she attributes to the Ouija board opening a gate through which those entities could pass. In one instance, when these mysterious events were happening, Lee lost consciousness suddenly and attacked a friend without reason before coming to. Lee believes she was possessed by one of the entities that was in the house.

In another instance, Lee and her friends were inside the house when all of the doors began opening and shutting in unison. All at once, the doors slammed and then locked. The frightened occupants of the house fumbled with the lock to a glass door, trying in vain to exit the house, but the lock stayed fast. Then, just as suddenly as they had slammed closed, all of the doors in the house opened at once, and everybody ran from the house. Lee knew where she was headed. She ran toward a ditch that they called the "army ditch." It was her childhood play place and a space in which she felt safe. But, before she could reach her hiding place, all of the fleeing kids were stopped dead in their tracks, as if rooted to the ground.

Unable to move her feet, Lee turned her head slowly with all of the rest, as they gazed back into the house through the glass door. The curtain lifted. Everyone present saw the same creature, memorable for its big eyes. Years later, Lee said that others in the neighborhood would report seeing the same creature gazing out of the house at another point in time.

Thirteen-year-old Lee did not tell her parents about what happened with the Ouija board, but her mom knew that something had happened. Lee's mom would feel something creepy watching her, but then would sense the smell of roses and feel safe. She blamed her daughter for getting up at night and turning the television on, but Lee knew it was actually the strange energies that she had let loose in the house. At one point, Lee remembers arguing with her mom, denying that she was turning on the television. As if to prove that Lee was not the culprit, the stereo turned on as if by magic and began blaring music. Hitting the buttons and even pulling the plug mysteriously would not turn off the music. Lee and her mother had to actually beg the stereo to end its madness before the music stopped.

The real moment that confirmed the haunting for Lee's mom was after Lee had a nightmare one night. Lee awoke, terrified, and called out for her mom. She ran from her bed and opened her bedroom door, shouting into the hallway desperately for help. When her mom emerged from her own bedroom, Lee was clinging to the doorknob but floating sideways in midair, as if hanging from the door. Lee's family was unable to deal with this level of haunting, so they decided to move.

As an adult, Lee visited her old neighborhood. She wanted her brother to come too, but he is frightened to this day that the entity in that house will recognize him and follow him home, so he declined. Lee returned to the old house and scrutinized the exterior, but nothing seemed amiss. When the current owners, a nice-looking couple, exited the house, she greeted them and cheerfully explained that it was her childhood home. They seemed very friendly, so she decided to ask them about her past. "This probably sounds like an odd question, but . . . has anything unusual happened here?"

The wife's face blanched. Immediately, the couple confessed to hearing stomping in the attic. They had seen things fly off the shelves and watched doors open and close on their own. The activity, they said, seemed centered around one room in the house in which noises issued from the closet and from behind its closed door. Lee knew that it was her old bedroom, the one in which they had summoned forth dark energies from the Ouija board. Unwilling to take the blame for what she had done, however, Lee cheerfully bid the current homeowners goodbye and left, never to see them or the old house again.

Space brothers

"Space brothers" is the politically correct term for aliens. A good friend of mine believes in space brothers so much that she actually integrates them into her spiritual experience. She believes that the space brothers are energetic beings that exist on an ethereal plane. Space brothers come to Earth so frequently that they form lights in the sky every night that change color and shape. My friend also believes that the space brothers are here to help and protect us by cleaning the atmosphere and the like.

So one day, my friends and I decided to have a space brothers party. My friend Tonya did the bartending, making us all some cosmos. Cielito brought a huge telescope and some movies about space brothers. Sarah brought chips and avocado dip in the shape of the head of a cartoonish alien. We played music that had to do with space travel and star-ships. We started a bonfire outside and relaxed to watch the sky, which had patchy clouds but a few clear spots. Listening to my friend's hopes of seeing space brothers made me smile, as she said that she could sometimes think of them and then see them. So, I suggested trying to contact the space brothers using my Ouija board.

The first two partygoers to sit down at the Ouija board immediately found space brothers present. "Are you here, space brothers?" they asked. The answer was "yes, yes, Ouija." Joking onlookers drinking cosmos leaned over the board with excitement, jabbering at the aliens and laughing glee-fully. The planchette whizzed around the board spouting gibberish and repeatedly pointing at the picture of the sun before moving to "goodbye."

"You guys," one of the Ouija board players protested, "the space brothers obviously don't like that you're laughing at them. I think they left." The planchette began to move more slowly and deliberately, pointing to the number 4, the letter U, and then sliding back into gibberish. "Are we talking to some-one other than the space brothers now?" The question had to be asked. The Ouija board spelled out "yes, RUN, yes. Wind. Goodbye." The players decided to end the session, pointing out that there was a markedly different feeling when everyone was laughing and making fun. "This is not a joke. It doesn't like all the laughing."

Another couple of players stepped up to the plate. One of them went by the name of Cosmik, and was someone whom I hadn't met before this party and who came with my friend Phoenix. Cosmik and Phoenix excitedly revealed that they were "Ouija virgins," having never before used the board to contact anyone, much less a space brother. They were overjoyed when the Ouija board indicated that the space brothers were back. The planchette zoomed all around while partygoers bickered and told those who were laughing at the space brothers to walk away from the Ouija board.

The space brothers, speaking through the board, indicated that they were very angry with the laughter and that they were feeling destructive. Phoenix even felt that there was a threat coming from the Ouija board. The planchette spelled out letters so quickly it was difficult to follow. "I met hub…" The Ouija board stopped making sense. Cosmik asked, "Why do you want to destroy Phoenix?" Suddenly the planchette stopped dead and refused to move, much to their surprise, as if it were stuck to something on the board.

The spooky slumber party

The first time I was invited to a co-ed slumber party as a young teenager, I was excited. It was going to be a birthday party at my good friend Lisa's house, and would involve sleeping in her backyard in huge tents, one for the boys and one for the girls. I packed some appropriate games for the evening, which included my tarot cards, a Magic 8-Ball, and my Ouija board. I knew that I would have to hide them from my friend's mom, who seemed pretty hysterical over occult things. Not me; I was in the thick of my obsessive teenage interest in all things magical and ghostly.

I arrived early to help my friend set up for her party and was too excited to keep my toys in my backpack. When I was surreptitiously showing them to my friend behind her mom's back, my friend's brother Sam caught sight of what we were doing. Sam scared me when I was thirteen years old. He was a few years older than us, very tall, and always dressed in black. Rumors abounded about Sam, which piqued my fears and intrigue.

A good friend of mine claimed that Sam had once witnessed a stabbing. His mom told us that he had set fire to his bed with a flare gun. Another group of kids at school claimed that Sam was dangerously insane and had broken furniture in a psychiatric home for kids when he was committed on his birthday. I realize now as an adult how wrong it was to fear a teenaged boy who was dealing with his own problems, but at the time I didn't know any better. Most intriguing of all, I knew that he also had a deep interest in the occult. The kids at school said that he was a Satanist who cast evil spells.

Sam looked over my games with an unimpressed expression. His eyes flickered up and met mine. "I can see your spirit animal," he said in the husky voice he used to seem spooky. Sam looked more ugly than scary in broad daylight. Pale and skinny, he had a prominent nose and scruffy hair that fell around his face. Its tips were dyed black, but you could see his natural brown hair at the roots. He wore eyeliner even at home and was always clad in a series of band T-shirts that were several sizes too large. He twisted the hem of his shirt with his fingers. His nails were painted black.

"Really?" I asked. I hoped that he would say that my spirit animal was a bat, my favorite animals. "Your spirit animal is a mouse," he said. I tried to hide my disappointment.

"You can't see the forest for the trees," he continued. "Your mouse spirit makes you too detail-oriented." I looked up at him again. That much did match my personality, and he didn't really know me. I realized that I didn't know him, either.

When it started getting dark, the other partygoers came, mostly kids from our school. Everybody was full of nervous energy, and I got uncomfortable right away. All of the painfully embarrassing young-teenager games were played, like "spin the bottle." I didn't feel like kissing some random boy that a bottle pointed toward, and the boy I liked wasn't even at the party, so I excused myself from the game and hung out near the edges of the room, trying to interest other people in the games I had brought instead. At some point, a critical mass of giggly partiers followed me outside the house and through the damp, dark grass toward a tent in the yard.

The tent where we would be spending the night was enormous. As a short girl, I could easily stand inside. There was even a divider set up in the tent. Lisa had argued that the boys could sleep in one half and the girls in the other, but her mother had insisted that the boys stay in a separate tent, as if a thin sheet of fabric was a barrier against teenaged mischief. A lone battery-powered lantern hanging from the ceiling provided the lighting. I set up the Ouija board and proudly explained to all of the participants how it was to be used. I selected two eager participants to be the first to use the game.

The tent continued to fill with kids as the "spin the bottle" game was abandoned. Sam even showed up with two of his gangly-looking older friends, though they were not invited to the party. Lisa briefly protested, telling her brother to get out of the tent, but in the uproarious noise of the party she gave up as she was ignored. I was doing some protesting of my own, because people weren't following the Ouija board rules. Instead of just two people sitting at the Ouija board at a time, multiple kids were leaning in to touch the planchette. In fact, I couldn't even see the board anymore, since everybody was shoulder to shoulder. People were shouting questions loudly at the board and squealing as the planchette moved. Those closest to the board called out the letters as they were highlighted.

At first, the questions were pretty typical of people our age. Girls were asking if boys had crushes on them. Boys were asking silly questions about when and how they would die. Not wanting to miss out on the fun, I shouted over the din, asking if there were any ghosts or other entities present. Sam added on to what I said, asking if there were any demons or spirits present. Suddenly, the wind outside the tent picked up. The party quieted down for a moment, listening to the harsh whisper of the wind slipping the ends of branches against the smooth material of the tent. With a snapping sound, the planchette flew straight up off the board, flipping through the air. Two pieces flew in different directions. A gasp arose from the crowd. "You were pressing too hard," a girl's voice complained.

"Something is here," Sam intoned in a booming voice. Abruptly, the battery-powered lantern dimmed and then went out. Chaos ensued. Several girls screamed. Several boys began making growling noises just to be obnoxious. Kids began pouring out of the tent. I followed Lisa, whose face looked troubled in the moonlight. She hugged her arms close around her. "Somebody touched me," she said. I shook my head in anger, figuring that some boy had taken the opportunity to cop an unwanted feel. Seeing my anger, Lisa said, "No, no. Somebody touched me who wasn't human. Its hands were ice cold and they touched the top of my head and my face."

I stared at her. My friend was pretty excitable, but she wasn't giggly and silly right now at all. She was uncharacteristically subdued, and that made me scared more than the flying planchette, the wind, and the lantern's batteries running out. The wind blew, icy and cold. Most of the kids moved back toward the house, muttering. I went too, but just to get a flashlight. Try as I might, though, I couldn't get anyone to agree to come back out to the tent with me to try to play with the Ouija board.

Even Sam seemed uninterested. I tried to convince him that I wanted just to go out and find out the name of the entity that was present. "I already know his name," Sam said loftily. "I summoned him during a ritual I performed in order to gain more occult power." I was interested, and pressed him for details.

"What is his name then?" I asked. "And what sort of ritual? Why did you perform it in the first place?" Sam just shrugged and rolled his eyes at his friends.

"I don't think you did a ritual at all," I countered. "I think that you just want to seem dark and scary to people, but I'm not convinced."

Sam's eyes narrowed at me accusingly. With a string of profanity, he left the house, his two friends following. They went through the front door, probably to walk to town and cause havoc. I felt vindicated, but part of me wondered whether he really had summoned something negative that was sticking around Lisa's house. With flashlight in hand, I returned alone to the tent. The lens had popped out of the planchette, but the pieces easily snapped back together. Seating myself at the Ouija board, I decided to ask the questions I wanted.

"Ouija, is some force causing negative energy here?" The planchette indicated that yes, there was. "Ouija, who did it? Who is causing the negative energy? What is his name?" The Ouija board spelled out the name of Lisa's brother, Sam.

Ouija board as doorway

Sometimes the most exciting stories about the Ouija board aren't those about what happened during the game, but about what happened after. Some believe the Ouija board is a doorway for creatures from another world, or the cause of an influx of bad luck. This story happened at my childhood home along with a friend of mine, Tori. We were both twelve years old and enjoyed playing with the Ouija board, mostly as a way to ask inane questions about boys.

On this particular Ouija board play session, my friend and I were camping in my backyard. My parents owned a tent trailer, which is sort of the best of both worlds between a tent and a camper. A hard lower shell extends out two shelves to act as beds, and a canvas tent makes up the rest of the structure. There was a hard door, but all of the sides were soft. It always rested on a gravel strip in the backyard, near the wooden gate, and when it was pitch black outside it was the perfect spooky place to use the Ouija board. The wind would whisper through the alder trees overhead, making it feel like we were deep in the woods, even though the warm house and bathroom were only fifty paces away.

That night, Tori and I were alone in the tent trailer with my cat, Confetti, an excitable spotted tabby kitten. We asked the Ouija board a million stupid questions. My friend was especially boy-crazy, so she had an endless list of names that she would go through, asking the Ouija board if each boy liked her. The planchette would dutifully indicate yes or no, sending her into a trill of contagious giggling. Eventually, I got bored with the line of questioning. Feeling tired and chilly, I wanted to snuggle into my sleeping bag and chat until sleep overcame us.

Tori reluctantly put all the games away that we had been playing, including the Ouija board, and we lay down to go to sleep. Tori was still wound up, however. "It feels weird," she said. "It feels like somebody is here with us." I didn't feel the weirdness that she felt, so I just snorted and shook my head. My eyes were not so heavy anymore, though. Thoughts began to creep through my mind. What if she was right? What if there was some sort of entity here, the same entity that was making the Ouija board talk to us? It could be spending the night in the tent trailer with us.

Just then, Confetti began acting very strangely. Resting where she was on my chest where she had settled down to sleep, I could feel her become very tense. In the dim light inside the trailer, I could see her fur puff up with fear or anger. A deep rumbling growl started low in her belly and escaped like a moan. Tori's voice came thin in the darkness. "What's wrong with Confetti? I've never seen her do that!"

"Neither have I," I admitted. My cat had spent countless nights out here in the tent trailer with me and had never been so frightened. The only things that frightened Confetti were dogs and other cats. Confetti had stalked off of my chest and was perched on the bed, flicking her puffed-up tail nervously and glaring out the side of the canvas toward the gate. The windows were zipped closed, so we couldn't see out. Even if they had been unzipped, we wouldn't have been able to see anything through the mesh into the darkness.

The gate creaked open loudly in the night. Was it just the wind? Confetti growled more loudly. "Who's there?" I asked. Tori had crept across from her bed and was now sitting on mine, her body tense. She whispered to me in the sort of whisper that only fearful people make, where very little breath escapes the throat. "Oh my god," she mouthed, "Something is there. Something's coming for us." It sounded nonsensical and I looked at her as she scooped up Confetti and held the cat close. It was then that I heard the footsteps.

Crunch. Crunch. Crunch.

Confetti growled even louder, her voice rising to a frenzied yowl. But this wasn't the sound of a dog, it was a human's footsteps. Tori and I stayed absolutely quiet. I allowed my breath to come shallowly so that I could hear more clearly. All I heard was the same rhythmic footsteps and some heavy breathing that mixed with the wind. Movement in the corner of the tent caught our eyes. The outline of a hand appeared in the darkness and fingertips trailed along the fabric of the tent.

The crazed cat yowled again, this time staring at the door of the trailer. I leaned in toward Tori, using the same breathless whisper that could only be heard an inch from her ear. "We have to get out of here. We have to run for the house. Are you with me?" Tori shook her head, clutching the growling cat. My mind was made up, though. I had to get out of this feeling of entrapment, at least to go get help. The back door to my house was a short run away up some wooden steps and across a deck. My parents were inside sleeping soundly.

I rose and crept silently toward the door. My cat craned her neck as if to see around me, as if she could see what was stalking us through the walls of the tent trailer. I hoped that I wouldn't collide with whatever was outside. My hand rested softly on the latch and I strained to listen to the sounds outside the trailer. I heard a crunch of the gravel on the far end of the trailer. This was my chance. I bolted.

My bare feet hit the gravel and I was flying in the sort of run that hurts your chest when you breathe too hard. The door to the trailer automatically slammed shut behind me. Simultaneously, I heard Tori's scream rising loud and clear from the trailer. I was already pounding up the wooden steps. My hand reached the sliding glass door of the house and I turned briefly to see if Tori was all right. She was still not visible inside the trailer. What was visible, however, was a shadowy figure that seemed too tall to be human.

I blew inside the house and rocketed down the hallway to my parents' bedroom. Throwing open the door, I shouted breathlessly, "Help! There's somebody outside." I struggled to find the words for the supernatural sort of fear that this thing engendered. My mom flicked on the lights and my dad calmly climbed out of bed, retrieving a gun from his bedside drawer. Always the pragmatist, he showed no signs of fear in the face of his hysterical daughter.

The three of us went outside. The gate was open, but the tall figure was gone. We could hear Tori sobbing loudly inside the trailer. My father shrugged and went back inside, not wanting my friend to see him in his underwear. My mother came inside the tent trailer to help us gather our things and go inside the safely locked house. She told us that it was just somebody coming to scare us, or perhaps some homeless person hoping that the tent trailer was an unoccupied place to crash. My friend Tori was not convinced, however. She believed the Ouija board drew that experience to us somehow. Whether it made us a target for a random night prowler or the presence outside the trailer was something more sinister, we'll never know.

conclusion

I hope you've enjoyed the intriguing and sometimes chilling stories from the previous chapter. Remember, all the stories are true tales, so if they frighten you, you have good reason to use caution around Ouija boards. If precautions aren't taken, you might end up scaring yourself silly at best, and possibly experiencing some negative paranormal activity at worst.

When I was in the process of writing this book, I had the pleasure of having many things summoned from the Ouija board in my home—everything from ghosts to giggles. I think the strangest phenomenon of all was that in writing this book, the book worked very hard to un-write itself. In fact, this book took much longer to write than the three other books I've written this year, some of them concurrently, and not because I was slacking off in my work.

Unlike all the other projects that I've put together, this book had several of what I could only guess were saving errors on two different computers. I thought it was the method I was using to back up my files, and I worked to solve the problem but to no avail. "The book is haunted," I said to my husband. I was exasperated at the lack of progress as my work was mysteriously deleted. It was as if I was taking one step forward, only to go two steps back. My husband, a computer guy in his own career, assured me that it was user error. He blamed one of my computers and one of the word-processing programs I was using.

However, even when I switched word-processing programs to the one my husband recommended and to the new and more powerful computer, the book still resisted progress. In fact, the problem grew even more mysterious when my work didn't even make it to the backup process because it wouldn't save locally. It was as if some power didn't want this book to be written. Undaunted, I've gone to great lengths to rewrite passages that have been repeatedly destroyed, working overtime to make this information available to you. My advice in this matter is to always keep notes about your Ouija board sessions as handwritten hard copies!

Hopefully the weird, true, and freaky stories about the Ouija board in this book have given you food for thought. It is easy to think that the Ouija board is just a game. However, Ouija boards, talking boards, planchettes, and related forms of divination have a long and proud history in varied faith traditions. It could be that the Ouija board is just speaking to our inner subconscious, allowing us to express things that surprise ourselves. However, in some belief systems it is thought that the Ouija board itself is a deceptively simple but powerful tool for spirit communication.

Even if the idea of spirit communication doesn't find a place in your belief system, you can still have plenty of fun and enjoyment with a Ouija board. Perhaps you can use the Ouija board to talk to your inner subconscious, or even to God. Conversely, if your religion forbids the use of the Ouija board, the stories in this book may have given you confirmation of why you should avoid using the Ouija board. For many people, the board has been a life-changing experience, though not always for the better.

If you do not have any belief system at all, you may find it silly that people have had traumatic experiences with the Ouija board, but chances are that you have rarely used it yourself. Regardless of what you believe, if you choose to explore the Ouija board, I hope this book has given you enough tips and techniques to protect your emotions and even your spirit while doing so. If you are playing with a Ouija board, you are playing directly with your mind and the minds of others, and possibly more.

It may be that many use the Ouija board without experiencing anything strange or frightening. After all, millions of children have played with the Ouija board and grown up to have only faint positive memories of childhood play. It is up to you to decide whether you want to make playing with the Ouija board a big deal for children who may find themselves in your care, or if you just want to let kids be kids. Consider strongly whether you can answer the question, "What's the worst that can happen?"

After all is said and done, the Ouija board is sold as a game. It is mass-produced by a large toy manufacturer and sold among other board games. Like a pencil or a hammer, the Ouija board is a tool has the potential to be used for fun, life improvement, or harm. The real magic is not found in the cardboard or plastic of the Ouija board, but within the hearts and minds of the people who give the Ouija board new life every dark evening.

bibliography

Buckland, Raymond. *Solitary Séance: How You Can Talk with Spirits on Your Own.* Woodbury, MN: Llewellyn Publications, 2011.

———. *The Weiser Field Guide to Ghosts: Apparitions, Spirits, Spectral Lights, and Other Hauntings of History and Legend.* San Francisco: Weiser Books, 2009.

Campanelli, Pauline. *Wheel of the Year: Living the Magical Life.* Woodbury, MN: Llewellyn Publications, 2011.

CNN Politics. "Obama Apologizes to Nancy Reagan for Séance Remark." CNN.com. November 7, 2008. http://articles .cnn.com/2008-11-07/politics/obama.seance_1_seances-first -lady-nancy-reagan?_s=PM:POLITICS

Danelek, J. Allan. *The Case for Ghosts: An Objective Look at the Paranormal.* Woodbury, MN: Llewellyn Publications, 2006.

New York Times. "A $59,285 Request by a Ouija Board Ruled Fraud Here." *New York Times.* March 3, 1970.

Righi, Brian. *Ghosts, Apparitions, and Poltergeists: An Exploration of the Supernatural through History.* Woodbury, MN: Llewellyn Publications, 2008.

Rowland, Ian. *The Full Facts Book of Cold Reading.* London: Ian Rowland Limited, 2008.

Sayed, Deonna Kelli. *Paranormal Obsession: America's Fascination with Ghosts & Hauntings, Spooks & Spirits.* Woodbury, MN: Llewellyn Publications, 2011.

Schirner, Markus. *Pendulum Workbook.* New York: Sterling Publishing Company, 1999.

Skinner, Stephen, and David Rankine. *The Keys to the Gateway of Magic: Summoning the Solomonic Archangels and Demon Princes.* Woodbury, MN: Llewellyn Publications, 2011.

Vanden Eynden, Rose. *So You Want to be a Medium? A Down-to-Earth Guide.* Woodbury, MN: Llewellyn Publications, 2008.

Please read on for an excerpt from
Crystal Ball Reading for Beginners,
another book by Alexandra Chauran

Hello, my name is Alexandra, and I'm the fortuneteller," I said as I arrived, toting my crystal ball, at the home of a woman celebrating her engagement, where she had gathered a dozen friends for an intimate celebration.

As I was ushered into her home, the comfortable clamor of friends excitedly talking became noticeably subdued as timid eyes sized me up. I was twenty-six years old, slender, and clad in a white dress. I entered the house barefoot, even though the weather had been brisk outside. Aside from my preferred barefoot state, there was nothing unusual about my appearance. My outfit was professional; my dark, shoulder-length hair was left in its naturally curly state, and my makeup and jewelry was minimal. I looked like just another guest.

I might easily have melted into the group's merry conversation over snacks if the guest of honor hadn't instructed me to let them know why I was there. I introduced myself to the group and gave a brief introduction to a type of fortunetelling called crystalomancy, explaining that, for people with problems with love or career, or any other area of life, divination offered practical solutions through the use of our intuition. I let them know that this evening I would be using a real crystal ball to confirm some things they already knew, to discover new potential in their lives, and to empower them with advice.

After such a bold speech, the guests were even more nervous. But the hostess allowed me to stick around and mingle while a few glasses of wine gave them courage. At last, the bravest of the bunch walked with me to a private area that the hostess had designated for readings, followed later by the rest of the excited guests once they had a chance to hear what she had to say about my reading. Over the course of the evening, I predicted children, extreme job changes, moves to distant lands, and even a few breakups to those who knew they needed to hear such news. By the end of the night, my table was crowded with everyone needing "just one more" reading.

How I Got Started

Teaching crystal ball reading is an unusual trade, even more so than telling fortunes using a crystal ball. In fact, I know of no others besides myself who currently offer local apprenticeships for learning how to perform this art. Though I learned how to read crystal balls at an early age with natural inclination, guidance from spiritual teachers, encouragement from parents, and a little bit of luck, it was only many years later that I began to pass on the knowledge that I've gained.

At first, with a bit of an ego, I assumed that I had special powers. But, given time and experience with others reading the crystal ball for me, I began to believe that everyone has the potential to practice this art. Some stumble upon their talents early; others must work hard on the discipline to achieve them; and still others actively work against developing such skills. My path in life has continuously drawn me into a teaching role, even when I struggled against it. With regard to the crystal ball, it began as a teenager when friends begged me to show them how I did it. An inability to understand how they might be different from me in their use of the crystal ball, as well as possibly a bit of self-sabotage in order to keep feeling special with my unique activity, kept us all frustrated for a while.

In college, I began to learn about psychology and the language of symbols that permeates all societies. Fascinated with how this was a common part of the human condition, and how it could be directly related to crystal ball reading, I hungrily studied symbols in many cultures and the common storylines that arose again and again. Just as I recognized the Hero's Journey in many stories, retelling the epic journey of someone going to another realm to bring back treasure, I realized that it was going to be my own task to bring back my own experiences from the crystal ball so that others could share in these universal understandings.

I learned that Carl Jung, the founder of analytical psychology, believed that the mind holds keys for how we work through problems in everyday life. The prominent psychologist used dream interpretation as a way to help people move through this world of symbols to understand how best to solve their own issues. Crystal ball gazing is very much like interpreting dreams that you are having while you are wide awake, and so it has the benefit of a deeper understanding of psychology.

Later thinkers, like mythologist Joseph Campbell, believed that symbols and archetypes found in repeating patterns in stories throughout history reflect the archetypes in the lives of real people. His catchphrase was "Follow your bliss." When you march along with the flow of your destiny, which is this theoretical structure that follows the archetypes in the Hero's Journey played out in mythology, it can seem like every challenge is lighter upon your shoulders. Understanding archetypes in the crystal ball can help you flow along your path more easily by pointing the way that is best for you.

For example, I often drive a long distance to visit my spiritual peers and elders. Others might find the traffic, gas money, and time to be frustrating enough to avoid training in this way. But for me, it's not really an issue. I'm following my bliss, and any challenge in the way seems relatively easy to overcome when I put my mind to it. However, if I was traveling all that way for, say, a dental appointment, I might whine about the traffic all the time, and even find it a reason to quit. Dental work isn't my bliss! Everyone's true desire is different, which is why you might see so many of your friends enduring relationship squabbles that would be a dealbreaker for you, while refusing to tolerate annoying aspects of partners that you find endearing and easy to overlook! Let's just say that following one's bliss is as easy as falling in love.

So, what if you don't know what your "bliss" is, or how to follow it? That's where the symbology of your dreams and the crystal ball can help when they are interpreted as a psychological aid. Although divination tools can and are used by many therapists, I often joke to my friends that, as a fortuneteller, "I'm like a therapist, only I actually help people." There are very real emotional and intellectual benefits to getting to know yourself through a crystal ball.

You see, your subconscious knows, but your subconscious isn't talking to you from the place of language and your left-brained cognition. Instead, your subconscious talks to you through symbols that you can see in the crystal ball. For example, when choosing between two lovers, a man might envision in the crystal ball a heart next to the woman he should choose, who would be best for him, even if his conscious mind hasn't been made up. He might also see some symbols that help him think about things he had not yet considered, such as how the second woman's goals might diverge sharply from his own, symbolized as her face surrounded by cars and material objects that he would not be able to afford to buy for her.

The crystal ball can also be used to examine someone's personality, and to correct emotional disorders in the exact same way as the Rorschach inkblot test is used. The Rorschach test is widely used by clinical psychologists to analyze personality, thought process, motivations, and conflicts, and I believe that the crystal ball would be an even more powerful tool for use by psychotherapists and their patients. It is like an infinite database of such inkblots, freeing the practitioner from the cultural bias and other sources of error that limit the Rorschach scoring systems.

The crystal ball can be used by both the spiritual and the nonspiritual as a psychological tool to access your subconscious through your right brain, to identify your problems and the solutions to those problems so that you can make choices to run your life. Even for the deeply religious, this process is still going on, adding an extra dimension to the usefulness of crystal ball reading.

I felt during my first experience of crystal ball reading, and still feel, that the crystal ball is a uniquely marvelous tool for divination, because it is like a direct window to one's own subconscious mind. The beginner doesn't have to force somebody else's system to make sense. Instead, the beginner can immediately start to piece together his or her own system and learn an internal language of symbols that have been building since birth, and maybe even before that. At the outset, that may seem the more difficult route, and in some ways it is more challenging since it involves constant growth and reevaluation. But, on the other hand, it requires less rote memorization, and better equips the beginner to transfer those skills to other forms of divination, or even to apply those skills to existing life experiences such as dreams or visions that might otherwise be troubling and confusing.

After graduating from college with a Bachelor of Science degree, I started to find out more about the learning process, the teaching practice, and how these could be applied to crystal ball reading. In my work toward my Master's degree in teaching, I learned that our current models for schooling were developed during the industrial era. With factories adding on new parts at each new stage, similar ideas for teaching students were adopted. Kids were assigned to grades, and at each new grade were subjected to new information that built upon the last grade. This process is called scaffolding, and will be used in this book. However, people are not factory parts, and everyone is not the same. Especially in a highly differentiated activity such as divination, where everyone's perceptions, interpretations, and even the beliefs that inform the two of those can be different, any classroom or book would be entirely insufficient.

As a result, to this day I still feel unable to successfully teach a "Crystal Ball 101"–style class with an entire room full of students, preferring instead that each of my students work at his or her own pace. Though I've published many smaller articles about spiritual development, this is my first adventure into the book-publishing world, and with its success I hope many others will follow. It is my hope that this book will be the next evolution in my teaching of this craft, and that it will initiate a whole new learning adventure in individual students all over the world. Thank you for being a part of my story about how I got started reading and teaching crystalomancy for beginners.

What Is a Crystal Ball?

Crystal gazing is the art of looking into a crystal ball to receive perceptions of the past, present, and future. Fortunetelling using a crystal ball, or crystalomancy, offers an opportunity to develop your divination skills to their natural limits with a tool that allows for easy transfer to other methods. The crystal ball itself is a pure crystal sphere, of any size, usually translucent and made of quartz. Crystal ball gazing can be a form of scrying, the practice by which literal or symbolic images are seen that are believed to have meaning and purpose. I chose the crystal ball as the subject for this book because I do believe scrying to be the best way to train natural intuitive abilities as they pop up, since it allows the most freedom of perception and the best way to get to know your own inner self through a divination tool. I also believe the crystal ball to be the best scrying tool for beginners, since it allows you to train yourself to scry with any tool, while giving possible added benefits of the properties of the crystal itself.

There are those who use the crystal ball without scrying. For this use, the crystal is used as a focal point to clear the mind for meditation, so that the information can be revealed through other means. This can be presented through the other senses, or simply arise as an understanding.

How Do You Scry with a Crystal Ball?

There are many who will find the systems of quiet receptivity and symbolic analysis in this book to be useful, including the divination beginner wishing to expand his or her repertoire of tools, or the natural psychic who can't seem to "turn off" visions or other purposeful perceptions and is desperately seeking a focus. This book does not pretend to be complete, and after reading it, you will not be guaranteed the ability to start your own fortunetelling business. No book can or should be the only resource for that, and I am still a staunch proponent of apprenticeships for that goal, but with this book you can expect guidance for beginning a personal practice of meditation and reading a crystal ball for yourself and others, if desired.

I began scrying naturally from my earliest childhood memories. As a rockhound child, picking up every quartz stone and frequenting gem shows with my parents, the use of small crystal spheres was an extension to this everyday practice. My parents were very encouraging of all my imaginative and spiritual pursuits, and my mother also practices divination. At the age of eighteen, I began selling readings professionally, using many different methods of divination—but scrying remains one of my favorites due to the unlimited freedom of what can be seen in the crystal ball. I currently have a large and growing client base, and I can't imagine not being a fortuneteller or not reading the crystal ball. I hope that others will share in the joy of my modern revival of this ancient art.

You, as the reader of this book, should have equal doses of faith and doubt. Expect to create a new language of symbols that may be partly a psychological science, and partly in the flexible realm of spirit and an evolving mythology. Along the way, mistakes and changes can be made, and that is okay. As Joseph Campbell wrote in his book *Myths to Live By*: "What would the meaning be of the word 'truth' to a modern scientist? Surely not the meaning it would have for a mystic! For the really great and essential fact about the scientific revolution—the most wonderful and challenging fact—is that science does not and cannot pretend to be 'true' in any absolute sense. It does not and cannot pretend to be final. It is a tentative organization of mere 'working hypotheses.'"[1]

History

The availability of other scrying media, such as fire and dark bowls filled with water, probably means that this practice

---

1. Campbell, *Myths to Live By*, 17.

predated the use of the crystal ball as a tool. Today, these older tools are still used, along with others. Scrying mirrors used in ceremonial magic are still used, and have found their way into modern folklore with ghost stories featuring mirrors and the fabled "Bloody Mary" appearing to frightened adolescents under specific circumstances such as Halloween, darkness, and the chanting of her name. Those with modern-day connections with Picts sometimes use a *keek-stane*, a darkened piece of convex glass set into a box or base.

The first users of crystals for divination were certainly religious. This early usage is attributed to the Druids, as early as 2000 BCE. Later, Scottish Highlanders used natural beryl for divination, valuing it for its transparent quality and replacing the beryl with more transparent crystals whenever possible. History and myth blur in medieval literature, where one finds crystal ball use by everyone from wizards to the Romani people.

Crystal balls have been used for séances since at least the eighteenth century. The setup of a traditional séance often used multiple family members around a table, holding hands or placing hands on the table with the little fingers touching, which allowed overwhelmed participants to pull away and reconnect with ease. A historical séance procedure compiled by Dr. Mark Mirabello, of Shawnee State University, suggests ritual objects similar to those that might be found in other Western magic circles, including a bell, rock salt, and a steel knife.[2] And a lily on the west side of the bowl, along with candles to the bowl's north and south.

---

2. See Mark Mirabello, PhD, "A Séance Procedure." PDF available online at http://www.markmirabello.com/seacuteance-procedure.html.

Later Christian influences to the largely Greek procedure included a Bible open to 1 Samuel, chapter 28, with a quartz crystal resting upon it. Incidentally, the Bible refers to crystal balls as shewstones. In Christian séances, having five people at the table was avoided, as it was believed that number of people would remind spirits too much of the five wounds that killed Christ.

If both meditation and scrying can be done with other, easier-to-obtain tools, why has the use of a crystal sphere persisted? Why did the Scottish Highlanders, who had an abundance of clear water, seek out the most transparent beryl that they could possibly obtain?

This book will lead you through the process of understanding not only what a crystal ball is and how to choose your own, but also the process of beginning to use the crystal ball to answer questions about love, money, and more. Step-by-step instructions will tell you what to look for and how to think about what you see. As you develop your skills with meditation, you will be guided to handle tricky interpretations with increasing ease—and even read for others, if that is your eventual goal.

Dive in to learn more about the ancient art of crystal ball reading and how it can help you.

How to Choose a Crystal Ball

A natural quartz crystal ball was once stolen from my person, a situation that makes me greatly concerned for the physical well-being of the thief and her family. (Be careful about buying a crystal from a pawn shop, as you never know what baggage it may bring home with you.) But it did cause my peers to rally around me to help me replace the lost divination tool, since they knew that this was how I made my living. I actually got wonderful results out of this bad situation, as I received two replacements—one the same size as the stolen sphere and one even larger.

The first replacement was the same size as the original and came from my spiritual teacher, Elder, and High Priestess. She had actually ordered several quartz spheres of that size from an online gemstone retailer prior to the theft, and I remember she had me come out to her car and choose which one I would like to have. As I lifted each one to the light, I asked each one which was right for me and looked for the answer. In one of them I perceived the letters in my name presented in order inside the crystal ball, as if it were spelling my name, so it was quite clear that was the one for me. I blessed it during our ritual that night and have used it ever since.

My second replacement came from my mother, who went to a gem shop. The gem-shop owner, upon being asked for a crystal ball, erroneously pointed my mother at first to some impressively large glass spheres. My mother politely explained that she was looking for real crystals, and was shown to the natural quartz spheres. As the shop owner was not familiar with crystal ball reading at all, she began to show my mother the largest crystal spheres, as those are the most expensive. However, even though my mother was prepared to buy me the biggest crystal in the place, if that was the right one, she could tell that many of the very largest crystals were unsuitable, having not enough natural inclusions to catch the light. The shop owner must have been disappointed to see her pass by an enormous and nearly flawless crystal to choose a slightly smaller one with more imperfections.

How My Crystals Came into My Life

Scrying in many objects was a personal spiritual practice for as long as I can remember, but even I was nervous about procuring my first actual crystal ball. After all, a real piece of crystal is quite the financial investment for a child, even one who was spoiled with a large allowance. I had also heard a rumor from tarot-reading friends that a deck of cards should not be bought, but should be given to you. Now, that isn't necessarily true, but I wondered at the time if it would apply to crystal balls as well, and whether I could manipulate this bit of lore in order to get myself a free crystal ball.

I needn't have worried, because my Aunt Sue is incredibly supportive of my divination arts, requesting readings herself at times, and also loves to buy me trinkets for no reason at all. And so, my first crystal ball was a small one, mounted in a necklace, toward which I merely had to point my finger and show the slightest interest to my aunt before she rushed to purchase it for me. I didn't even have to begin my well-rehearsed story about why it was important. I also rationalized to myself that, if it somehow didn't work, I could simply wear it as a piece of jewelry. Of course, it did work just fine, and I still use it to this day, as a way to inconspicuously carry around a crystal ball.

My mother has also been a professional fortuneteller, and although she is retired now, she still offers her talents at fundraisers and for family and friends. She has purchased several crystal balls for me, and she always has an eye for those that fit the right specifications. The two of us love to talk shop about performing readings, and we even had a chance to work side by side on a cruise to the Bahamas with a "psychics on the sea" theme!

Once I started using my first crystal ball, I was hooked. Surely, some of my initial motivations for trying it out had to do with simply being involved in this ancient art that was recognized in a very widespread way, and yet so mysterious to all involved. Once I tried it out, I was surprised at how easy it was.

I had imagined squinting my eyes at a clear sphere and giving up after not being able to make out a thing. But as the images and symbols were easily found in the rainbows and shiny sparkles inside even my tiny crystal ball, I was hungry for more. I must admit, thought, that my desire for additional and larger crystals was also because it might be more impressive than gazing into a tiny marble.

My next crystal ball came to me as a birthday present from a friend and client, who knew of my interest in divination of all sorts. It was small also, one and a half inches in diameter, but was wonderful for travel. It came in a small, velvet bag, and is still the crystal I bring with me when going on a trip by car or plane, since it is unlikely to get broken when wedged deep in my clothing bag. I do choose to use this slightly larger crystal ball over my necklace when traveling, when I don't have to be discreet—not because it is more effective, but simply because it is easier to allow light into a larger crystal while holding it, since your fingers don't block off a large percentage of the surface area. The same friend and client later gave me an amethyst crystal sphere of the same size that, while good for healing readings, I do not often use, because the purple hue can obscure some of the other colors that might come through in my readings.

My next steps up in crystal collection and size were crystal spheres about three inches in diameter, given to me by my mother and my spiritual teacher. I find this size to be ideal for most cases, because it is large enough that there are many small imperfections inside to examine and small enough that it fits into the palm of one hand to be turned easily and exposed to the light. I find this size and larger is the size for which I most often reach. It can also fairly easily travel in a purse, though one has to be careful not to knock the bag against anything.

My largest crystal ball, about four inches in diameter, is the one I use at home. Its size is impressive, so I certainly bring it to events at which I will be on camera, but I do worry about dropping or breaking it in transit due to the fact that it must be handled with two hands and is somewhat more heavy. At any rate, regardless of size, any crystal ball has advantages over more organized divination systems due to the ease of scrying and the freedom and diversity of what can be seen.

What to Look for

Before you select your first crystal ball, it is important to decide for what purpose you would like to use it. If you intend to attempt to see visions in it at all, transparency is key. Thus, for your first crystal, the best choice may be a natural quartz crystal sphere. You're looking for a sphere that overall is so clear that, when holding it in your hand, you should be able to clearly see the color of your fingers. However, an entirely clear ball is not what you want. Look for small "inclusions," or tiny flaws within the crystal that will look like flat, rainbow, three-dimensional effects. Clear, lead crystal is unsuitable due to its lack of flaws. The ideal crystal ball will have countless inclusions but be otherwise clear. Some cloudiness is okay, but not so much that it obscures your inclusions.

If you are absolutely sure that you do not want to attempt to see visions in the crystal and only wish to use it for meditative and trance purposes, then you have a lot more freedom and can choose an opaque crystal, transparent or translucent. I find that, for this purpose, a more shiny crystal of a very consistent hue can be best. The shine of the crystal can create optical illusions that allow you to better soften your focus, and a lack of color variation does not tempt your mind to be distracted by perceived shapes.

As for the size of your crystal ball, size is truly not the most important factor. I used to joke when I was first getting into crystal ball reading, upon discovering the expense of large, quartz spheres, that I wanted to start a rumor that the smaller the crystal ball was, the more accurate it was. This has not proven to be true in my experience. At the time of this writing, my smallest quartz crystal sphere is one centimeter in diameter and my largest crystal sphere is ten (about four inches). I switch sizes between readings without any further thought than travel considerations.

Beyond clear or white quartz, there are a myriad of gemstones that can be used, as long as they can be made to conform to a spherical shape. There are correspondences that can be used for many purposes, and I encourage you to experiment. A reader might choose to use his or her birthstone, or even of the month in which the reading is taking place.

Here are some examples of stones or colors that can be used. For Aries readers, or for the month of March, a carnelian sphere or any red crystal can be used. Aries was also the god of war, so readings or meditations over conflicts and anger or impulsive actions may be aided. Mars is also associated with the color red and with Aries. Tuesday, once called *Tyr's Day*, can be the most auspicious time to work with these correspondences.

For Taurus readers, carnelian, which is related to the month of April, can also be a useful gemstone. However, any stone of the color indigo can also work well. Gemini or the month of May can be associated with topaz, which can come in many hues, so if you can find one that is purple, that would be best. Cancer or the month of June corresponds with the gemstone chalcedony, or any crystal that is maroon in color. Readings for Leo or July would find Jasper or the color purple to be most auspicious. Virgo or August can use emerald, or any slate-gray gemstone. Libra or September can make use of the fabled beryl, or a stone of the color blue. Scorpio or October has the amethyst crystal ball, or any brown crystal sphere. Sagittarius or November works best with the hyacinth stone or any yellow crystal. Capricorn or December can use the chrysoprase gemstone or a black crystal. Aquarius or January works well with any sky blue crystal sphere, and Pisces or February can use a sapphire sphere or any tan-colored stone.

No matter what is going on in the world, love is always foremost on the minds of many, so I'd recommend a green crystal ball for love questions. If the questions have more to do with career, a black stone is good for one with a strong sense of organization—but if you have to take the lead, a blue one may work better. Health readings can be done with purple crystals. I know a healer who uses an amethyst crystal ball for all of her health readings, as was advised by author and healer Uma Silbey in her book *Crystal Ball Gazing*. As for those questions that deal with the dead, I still have best luck with white or clear crystals, which are also associated with the moon.

You may wonder about the convention of the spherical crystal. While people do use gazing crystals of all shapes for meditation and scrying, this obviously departs from the practice of crystal ball reading. I do believe that the sphere is the best shape for scrying and meditation, because it allows you to rotate the crystal in your hands freely while keeping the distance from the surface to the occlusions within the crystal ball relatively the same. You also have the added benefit of allowing the optical illusion of the images in the room being projected upside down to your eye by the lens effect of the light refracting, in order to help your visual focus and your mental trance. If you gaze into any convex lens, such as the side of a sphere facing toward you, you will see your own reflection upside down. If you gaze into any concave lens, such as the surface of the sphere farthest away from you if you look through the crystal ball, light can create an image to form just in front of the lens.

Every once in a while, some enterprising person comes up with another shape of crystal or another material that they proclaim is best for scrying. This is similar to diamond jewelry retailers who come up with their own patented diamond cut. The funny thing about that is that the round diamond cut is mathematically the best for the properties of any diamond to display the diamond's light refraction to the human eye. For this reason, all diamond certifications have to be performed on round-cut diamonds, and the round cut has endured through many a patented fad cut. Likewise, the sphere-cut shape of a crystal presents its ideal properties for scrying.

What to Avoid

My one request is that you please don't use just a glass sphere. Though I'm not knocking any other scrying tool, glass spheres cannot, by definition, be used for crystal ball gazing. Even though they can be very impressive, as cheap ones can be purchased that are great in size, such spheres diverge away from crystal ball use into another form of scrying, and if you are to experiment with this form of divination, I'd ask you to stay true to the tool. The reason that the use of glass spheres is a bit of a pet peeve of mine is because, as a crystal ball reader, you are an ambassador for this enduring art—and family, friends, or clients who see you use glass spheres and mistake it for crystal ball reading may develop misconceptions. I also think that going for size over possible substance is choosing theatricality over practicality, which isn't the purpose of this book.

Where to Find Your Crystal Ball

This is not something that you should order from a catalog or online, if at all possible. However, there is something to be said about just starting as soon as possible with the materials at hand and buying a better version later. Visit a local metaphysical bookstore or gem shop and ask about what you want. Just remember that the old standby is a quartz crystal with the properties that are outlined in this chapter for scrying. Move to the correct section of the store and pay attention to what feelings draw or repel you. If you've made good use of your intuition in the past, hold each stone in your hands before purchase and use your gut feeling to select the one that is right for you.

How to Care for It and Store It

Once you've selected your crystal or crystals, there is no one set of instructions for their proper care and feeding. I've not yet broken a crystal ball, myself (knock on wood), but due to the nature of the inclusions being of a different density than the rest of your crystal ball, it is important to avoid exposing your crystal ball to extreme temperatures or physical trauma. If you do plan to use your crystal ball in a spiritual context, you can bless it through your own spiritual tradition. I blessed mine in a magical circle during an appropriate time. If you have a regular space that you can use for meditation and trance work, your crystal ball can be placed there on a stand. I keep mine on a family altar, to which my husband adds objects that we find have spiritual meaning to us.

The material of the stand does not matter too much, although some magic circles avoid the use of silver, as that is reserved for the Goddess, or the use of iron, as that is believed to ward off some fairies. I have stands made of plastic and stands made of wood. It is important that the stands not be distracting, so there should not be carvings or decorations on the stand that distract your eye from the crystal.

Many lighted stands are available for purchase that make the crystal ball look quite lovely. I even own one of those with a light that changes colors. I bring it with me to fairs and festivals so that passersby will be drawn to the beauty of the shifting colored light as it shines up through the crystal ball on my table. Though you are welcome to use such lighted stands when your crystal ball is just on display for ornamentation, I do not find them to be at all useful during reading, and I do turn mine off, probably quite anticlimactically, when a client is ready for a reading. One that changes colors would be distracting from trance work and would mask any colors that emerge through your own perception of the crystal's qualities.

I even find that just a white lighted stand is not as good as using external overhead lighting, candles, or natural light. The harsh glare can tend to obscure the natural inclusions for me. Ideal lighting for me while scrying is indirect sunlight or a full-spectrum overhead light, while the best lighting for me for simple meditation is candlelight, just to help me get into a relaxed mood.

One last note about lighting is to avoid direct sunlight when working with your crystal ball outdoors. From personal experience, I can tell you that a crystal ball in direct sunlight acts like a magnifying glass burning ants, except that it refracts unpredictably within the natural crystal to allow the focused heat to beam out at a random location. I would never have thought of this until I had a photo shoot with a crystal ball in the sunlight and noticed a burning sensation on my hand as I held the crystal. Beware of starting a fire. It turns out that in addition to metaphorical *chi*, or "energy"—which is the phenomenon that connects the universe and manifests love, life, and change—you must be aware of how very real radiant energy reacts within your crystal.

Note that you can own several crystal balls for different purposes. You can switch freely between them, even during one reading. Some practitioners are careful to thank their crystal ball, as if it were a person, before switching to another in order to explain to the crystal ball that it will be asked for help again in the future. This anthropomorphism may help you feel as though you're developing a rapport with your crystals, but it can also be omitted if you feel that it is silly.

Be aware, though, that some practitioners believe that their tools take on very real personalities, and can be offended in a way that affects their use. It is a well-known legend that stolen divination tools can tend to create negative effects in the lives of the thieves. I know a reader who has a crystal for each reading topic she does, and rather than choosing a crystal for each purpose, she believes that the crystals seemed to select themselves as one began giving greater detail for her during love readings and one seemed to give more information during readings about conflict. If you will be using your crystal ball to attempt to speak with the dead, then you should know that in many traditional religions, such as that of the Yoruba people, it is believed that ancestors can get in the way of proper divination, and indeed many other aspects of life, if not properly honored and respected. Animism, which can include the thought that even crystals have souls, is a part of many traditional Native American religions.

It is proper etiquette not to touch the divination tools of another person, something that can certainly be applicable for a crystal ball, and not only for the obvious reason that somebody could drop and break it or smudge it. If you believe in the life energy of *chi* (and even if you don't), the possibility exists that someone could purposely or accidentally ground the carefully developed, nurtured, and stored *chi* that is within your crystal ball. One might also rub off personal *chi* that you do not want inside your crystal ball, including emotional baggage or ill intent. Foreign *chi* has the potential to alter the way your crystal ball works, if only very slightly, which can slow your own learning time as you work to develop a personal rapport with your specific crystal ball.

On the other hand, there may be some benefits to other people handling your crystal ball if you choose to read for other people. The *chi* that rubs off onto the crystal from the person for whom you are reading may be able to better allow symbolism that is significant to them to come through. Every person who handles your crystal ball might add their own *chi* and symbolism to it, expanding its repertoire and also your own. Thus, the best solution for you to reap these benefits may be for you to have at least two crystal balls, one that you can allow others to handle and the other that is off limits. I would suggest that the larger and more expensive of the two be the one that only you are allowed to touch.

If you must store your crystal ball out of sight, you can keep it wrapped in black cloth or in a black bag, as is traditional for many divination tools. During transit, I carry mine in a padded box. In case you're wondering: yes, I have successfully taken a crystal ball in my carry-on luggage when traveling by plane. At one point, when my carry-on was scanned by the x-ray machine, a curious airport official did take my crystal ball out of my bag and ask me what it was, followed by his taking out my tarot cards and sorting through them, one by one, to make sure that I hadn't stashed anything nefarious among them. My other divination tools must have been less threatening, as they were left undisturbed.

You may wear your crystal ball, if it is a small one. In fact, my smallest crystal ball, the one that is just a centimeter in diameter, is mounted as a pendant, wrapped in a silver claw loosely so that the crystal can still freely move within the claw. If you do choose to wear your crystal ball, make sure that the mounting of it does not interfere with lighting, visibility, or the ability for the crystal to rotate. That said, wearing your crystal can be a great idea. Not only is it a beautiful conversation piece, but the properties of the gemstone—protective, healing, or otherwise—may also be imparted to you. Moreover, you have the added benefit of always having your crystal ball with you, should you have a need to meditate or scry with it.

Before you begin to meditate or scry with your crystal ball, you may wish to do some preparation of it. This has two benefits. One, if you believe in *chi*, is to clear it of any negative *chi* and imbue it with the proper *chi* aligned with your intentions. The other benefit is purely psychological. That is, if you allow yourself to only use the crystal ball with the intent to depart from everyday life, it will more easily allow you to get into that mind state. So, finding ways to designate your crystal as anything but ordinary can help engender that respect for your purpose.

Cleansing or clearing is the most important step in this process. Similar to what I described in the story at the beginning of this chapter, it is possible that some very negative *chi* may have come along with your crystal. If you're not familiar with working with *chi*, you can cleanse your crystal physically with water, and then bury it in a box full of salt for a moon cycle to achieve good effect. If you are already familiar with visualization techniques and prayer, you can visualize light and color from your crystal's potentially sordid past flowing harmlessly out of the crystal and into the earth, praying for it to go away and be converted by the earth into more positive stuff.

To consecrate or charge the crystal ball to your purpose, you can also use prayer and visualization—this time praying for it to help you receive the messages you need to get, and visualizing color and light flowing up from the earth and into your crystal ball, representing the power you will require. If you are unfamiliar with working with *chi*, your crutch for charging your crystal ball can be sleeping with it underneath your pillow, if possible, for a moon cycle, or allowing it to be exposed to full moonlight. You can also touch it to representations of the four elements— incense for air, water, fire, and salt for earth—to help bless it.